SPECTRUM SCIEN[CE]

Exploring LIFE AND THE ENVIRONMENT

For National Curriculum levels 1-3

Graham Peacock, Robin Smith and Dave Kirkby

CollinsEducational

Published in 1992 by
CollinsEducational
An imprint of HarperCollins*Publishers*
77-85 Fulham Palace Road
Hammersmith
London W6 8JB

ISBN 0-00-310230 0

Edited by Valerie Fawcett, Syntagm Ltd.,
Abingdon
Designed and illustrated by AMR, Basingstoke
Printed by Martin's of Berwick Ltd
Bound by Hunter and Foulis, Edinburgh

Contents

Almost all the activities can also be used to promote skills of exploration at the appropriate level in AT1. Most activities provide opportunities for work at a range of levels and the teacher's notes indicate that range. They also show other attainment targets to which the activity is relevant.

Introduction

Using Spectrum Science

This book is one of a set of two dealing with National Curriculum science in key stage 1. Together they provide activities that cover the whole programme of study and the spread of attainment targets from levels 1 to 3. A similar set covers the programme of study for key stage 2 at levels 2 to 5.

Each book is organised around a cluster of related attainment targets. Book 1, Exploring Life and the Environment, deals with those parts of the programme of study concerned particularly with living things and the environment. Each double page spread has a page of teacher's notes and a photocopiable pupils' page. The pages progress through the levels for each attainment target in turn. Opportunities for teaching aspects of AT1 are identified in the table on each teacher's page.

The books have been written to assist busy teachers planning their science teaching. Therefore they relate closely to the programme of study and the statements of attainment which teachers need to address as they plan teaching and assessment.

They can be used:
a) as a basis for planning a scheme of work for years 1 and 2
b) to supplement existing schemes
c) as a source of ideas for activities to match to your pupils

To help with planning there are charts at the beginning of the book to assist you:

Contents: the subject of the activity and the relevant attainment target
Cross-curricular links: opportunities for linking the science activities with topics and themes across the curriculum
Resources: the resources and apparatus that will be needed for each activity

Managing science activities in the classroom

Practical advice on the management of the activities is given in the teacher's notes. Although many of the activities are best carried out by small groups, the notes do not assume that teachers have only a small group to teach. Suggestions for work with a class are included where appropriate, and activities are designed so that teachers do not have to spend excessive time with a few children.

The activities may be organised in a number of ways. You could carry out some of the work with the class as a whole. For example, activity 28 could begin with a visit to a plant nursery and production of a big book. Activity 29 could start from singing songs about the weather as a class.

You could give out related cards to several groups. For example, make a selection of the activities on plants and growing so that some children are observing and drawing while others make simple habitats. Another group could carry out investigations of seeds to follow up later.

You could use individual pupil pages as part of an integrated day. For example, have one or two groups working on activities 10 or 11 while other groups work on language and maths activities, use play areas or paint.

However you organise your children's science, you will want to balance the tasks so they do not all require your involvement at the same time. Some of the activities in this book enable children to work independently once they have been given the materials and a little guidance: for example, activities 8, 23, 29, 33, and 37. Others may follow on from class topics without needing any new instructions: for example, activity 21. In some cases it will be helpful to join the children during the activity to discuss and extend their ideas: for example, activity 20. In others you can talk with them afterwards about how to communicate their work: for example, activity 32.

In this book there are a number of activities focused upon the collection and observation of plants and animals in the classroom. This enables children to learn at first-hand about the needs and characteristics of living things. It also provides important opportunities for children to learn appropriate procedures both for hygiene and for the proper maintenance of living things. For further advice on this and other aspects of safety in school science, teachers are advised to consult a booklet produced by The Association for Science Education called *Be Safe!*

Cross-curricular Links

The activities at key stage 1 reflect the character of infant education. They emphasise first-hand experiences and play as a basis for learning about the world in a scientific way. Stories and games, visits and use of the local environment are indicated. The activities are related to topics and themes common in early education.

Opportunities for teaching cross-curricular themes and skills are indicated in the Cross-curricular Links chart. Observation by pupils features throughout and the activities are designed to extend their skills of scientific observation.

Resources

Each page of teacher's notes details the equipment needed in that activity. Items such as paper and pencils which are normally to hand are not listed. However basic equipment such as scissors or glue are indicated so that teachers know they will be needed during the activity.

The things you may have to get together for the activities are listed in the Resources chart. You can see at a glance which activities children can do with a particular resource. Resources that can be used to extend the activity are not included but are shown in the relevant teacher's notes.

Using the Teacher's Notes

Referencing the National Curriculum

On each teacher's page there is a table which indicates programme of study and levels of attainment for each activity.

PoS	Level	AT1			AT
		i	ii	iii	
	1				
	2				
	3				
	4				
	5				

PoS   Refers to paragraph number of the programme of study.

AT1   Coded by level and statement of attainment.
i, ii, iii refers to the following strands:
i) ask questions, predict and hypothesise;
ii) observe, measure and manipulate variables;
iii) interpret results and evaluate scientific evidence.

AT   The last column refers to the main knowledge focus by attainment target, level and statement of attainment.

Geography   Where appropriate reference has been made to statements of attainment in Geography in the National Curriculum. This is indicated by a 'G' in the last column followed by the number of the appropriate Attainment Target.

Apparatus

Lists essential items
(apparatus for extension activities is indicated)

△ Teaching notes give guidance on how to organise the activity and make the most of it, including:
any practical points or safety matters;
suggestions for setting, linking to play, topic or cross-curricular work;
guidance on developing the activity and probing or promoting pupils' ideas and skills;
language and communication arising from the activity;
📖 suggestions for ways pupils can record their work.

Science background

Background knowledge at teacher's level concisely presented.

QUESTIONS ⊘ EXTENSIONS ⊖ ASSESSMENT Ⓐ

⊘   Indicates questions you might use during the activity.

⊖   Suggests ways of extending the activity and challenging pupils or linking with other work.

Ⓐ   Gives ideas to help teacher assess pupils' understanding or skills. Assessment is seen here as something done in the course of pupils' normal classroom activities. However a focus is needed and the suggestions here should help teachers plan the formative classroom-based assessment that the National Curriculum requires.

Using the Pupils' Sheets

The pupils' sheets use as few words as possible and give guidance and stimulus through pictures. They can be photocopied and given to pupils along with any materials indicated in the teacher's notes on the facing page. It is always best to try out any activities you set for children.

Each activity is designed to be self-contained and lead to success for pupils as well as contribute to their science learning. Some activities inevitably require more extended observation, for instance in observing growth or change over time. Examples of how results may be recorded are shown on some pages to prompt the children.

The activities have been chosen so that children will not need constant attention or close direction. However you will still need to give some assistance and make use of opportunities for teaching and assessing their progress. Where teacher supervision is needed for safety or to make the most of the activity, pupils are directed to seek it at that point.

We have sought to achieve an appropriate balance between encouraging children to bring their own ideas to the activities and the guidance necessary to help them understand the purpose of the activity.

Resources

Resources	Activities where they are used
a *Equipment for observing, measuring and collecting*	
containers	3, 4, 25, 36, 38
droppers and pipettes	33
funnels	38
magnifiers/hand lenses	1-4, 6, 7, 12, 13, 16, 17, 24, 33-36
measuring beakers	38
microscope	36, 39
mirror	18
netting and rubber bands	4
plant pots and saucers	28, 39
plant spray	17
plastic spoons	3, 4, 37
timer	38
torch	17
transparent containers	1, 16, 24, 36, 37
trowel	36, 39
tweezers	9
b *other classroom equipment*	
balls	30
beads and threads	20
clipboards	27
hoops	24
plastic bottles	23, 24, 30, 40
staples, drawing pins, coins and cutlery	26, 35
syringe or bicycle pump	40
tape recorder	32
c *materials to collect*	
fruits showing seeds	12
iron nails	26, 35
leaves/twigs	7, 9
moss	3, 4
photos of babies and people at different ages	15
pictures of plants	11
pieces of food	24
plant labels/lolly sticks	6, 25
pot plants	2
rocks and stones	3, 4, 33-36
seed catalogues	6
seed packets	6, 13, 28
seeds and seedlings	5, 39
small animals	1, 4, 8, 16, 17
small plants	3, 4, 6
soil or compost	3-5, 13, 25, 28, 35-39
wrappers, litter, waste	22-25

Cross-curricular Links

Activity Number	Information technology	Health Education	Our environment	Litter	Gardens	Soil/Rocks	Weather	Seasons	Growth	Change	Animals	Ourselves	Food	Plants	Water	Opposites	Trees	Movement	Air
1					●						●								
2			●											●	●				
3			●		●				●	●									
4			●								●		●						
5									●	●				●					
6	●								●	●				●					
7			●		●				●					●		●			
8	●										●								
9			●	●			●		●	●				●			●		
10												●							
11					●									●					
12									●				●	●					
13						●			●	●			●	●					
14		●							●			●							
15									●			●							
16											●		●						
17											●						●		
18												●				●			
19								●				●							
20												●							
21										●	●								
22			●	●															
23			●	●												●			
24			●							●			●						
25		●	●	●		●				●			●						
26										●					●				
27			●	●						●				●					
28			●	●	●		●	●		●				●				●	
29						●				●									
30						●				●								●	
31						●				●									
32							●			●									
33	●					●										●			
34	●					●										●			
35						●				●									
36				●		●					●			●					
37				●		●													
38				●		●													
39						●								●					
40																			●
41		●										●	●						
42							●	●		●						●			
43			●	●			●	●	●					●			●		
44			●			●								●					
45							●	●		●									
46			●							●									
47																●			
48			●							●									

ACTIVITIES

1 Naming of parts

Naming parts of the human body
Assembling pictures of people

Apparatus

Large pictures of people cut from magazines
Glue and spreaders

PoS	Level	AT1 i	ii	iii	AT 2
2i	1		a		a
	2				
	3				
	4				
	5				

- Play games with the class (e.g. 'One finger, one thumb', 'Simon Says'). Introduce more parts of the body gradually.

- Pop-up-toys or puppets can be used to reinforce the learning of names. The activity sheet can be photocopied or enlarged or put on overhead transparency to focus attention on details and encourage the accurate use of terms.

- Children can cut up large pictures of people from magazines to make their own Jack-in-the-Box pictures or sequences.

- In all these activities children should be encouraged to develop a more precise vocabulary and relate pictures to the real human body.

Science background

Some terms are very specific (e.g. thumb, elbow). Some are used more loosely (e.g. chest, tummy/stomach). Some body parts (e.g. eye, head) can be seen easily in all sorts of animals as well as humans.

QUESTIONS ⑦ EXTENSIONS ⊖ ASSESSMENT Ⓐ

⑦ Point to your —

⑦ Where does the arm join the body?

⑦ What do we call this?

⊖ Explore how parts of the body are joined and introduce the skeleton.

⊖ Make puppets by joining parts.

Ⓐ How many parts of their own body can children name?

Naming of parts

Here comes a Jack-in-the-box.

Which parts of Jack's body can you see?

Which parts don't you see?

Make your own Jack-in-the-box picture.

SPECTRUM SCIENCE

Exploring Life and the Environment levels 1-3

2 Plant pictures

Making plant collages
Recognising and naming parts of plants

Apparatus

Range of collage materials
Scissors
Glue
Paper, card or cloth backing
Variety of plants in the classroom or nearby
Large pictures of plants which show parts clearly (including low
and tall ones, some with woody stems, some with flowers and
others without)

PoS	Level	AT1			AT 2
		i	ii	iii	
2i	1		a		a
	2				
	3				
	4				
	5				

- This activity can be linked with other investigations of plants (e.g. see activities 3, 4, 7, 9, 15, 16). It could arise from gardening, looking at a verge or patch of weeds, visiting a garden centre or examining plants brought into the classroom.

- Have contrasting plants available for children to refer to. Encourage them to examine and describe some. Introduce key terms a few at a time: leaves, flowers, buds, fruits, seeds, roots, stems (stalks, branches). Put the terms on large labels for children to use.

- Help children to choose appropriate materials to cut parts and assemble plants. Discuss how they will arrange the parts before they stick them down.

Science background

Leaves trap energy from light. They are mostly green but come in a variety of shades, shapes and sizes. They are arranged in different combinations on stems which support both leaves and flowers. Some stems are woody to make them stronger. Roots anchor plants and carry water to stems. Some buds become leaves; some become flowers.

QUESTIONS ⑦ EXTENSIONS ⊖ ASSESSMENT Ⓐ

⑦ Where are the roots on this plant?

⑦ How many leaves are there?

⊖ Look for flowers and fruits on trees or shrubs.

⊖ Look at various vegetables (whole plants if possible) and discuss which parts of the plants we eat.

Ⓐ Can children find the parts on new or unusual plants (e.g. grasses or water plants)?

Plant pictures

Make a plant.

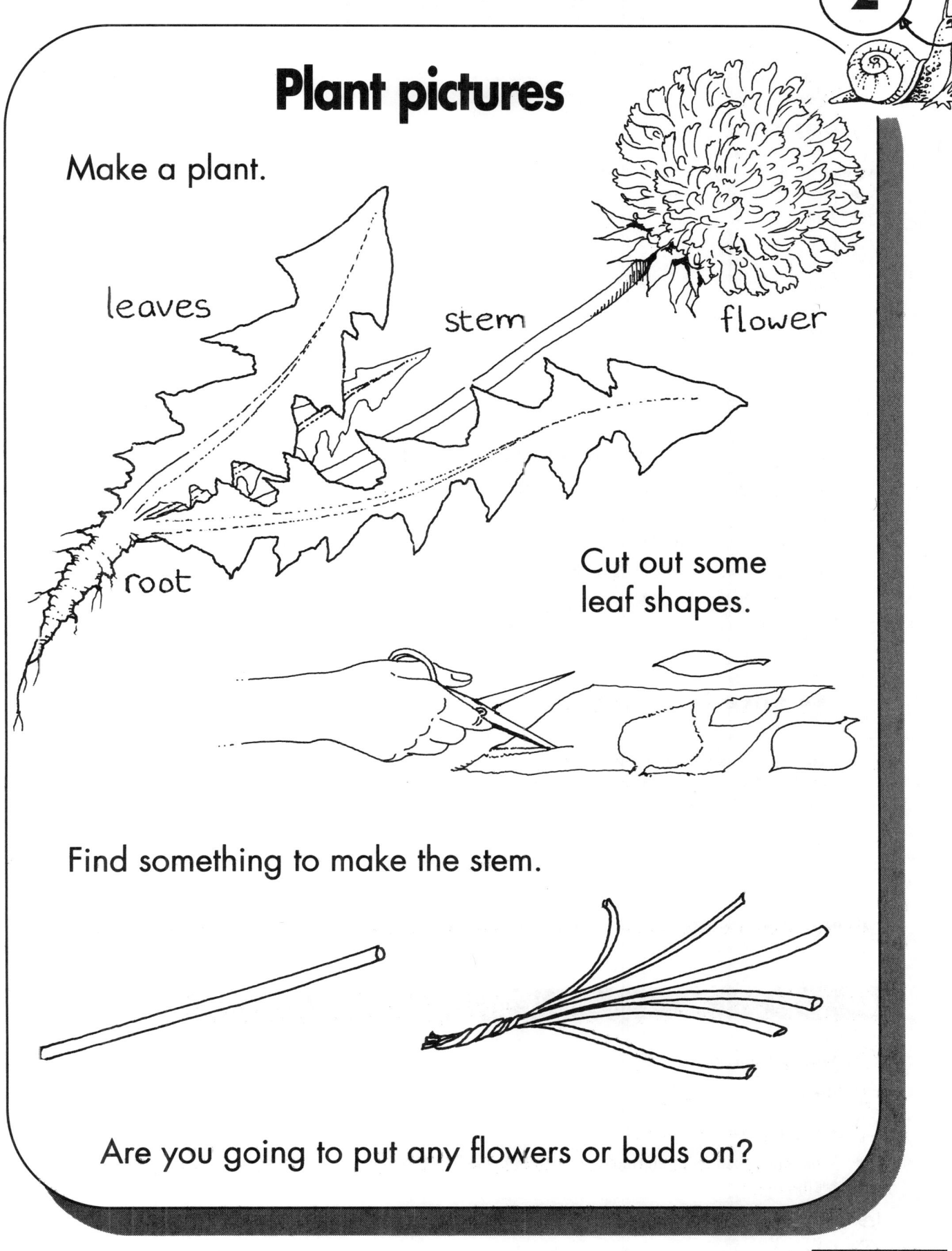

leaves

stem

flower

root

Cut out some leaf shapes.

Find something to make the stem.

Are you going to put any flowers or buds on?

SPECTRUM SCIENCE

Exploring Life and the Environment levels 1-3

3   All sorts of plants

Observing a variety of plants

Apparatus

A range of plants in pots, including non-flowering plants like
ferns, and at least one in flower
Hand lenses

PoS	Level	AT1 i	ii	iii	AT 2
2i	1		a		b
	2				
	3				
	4				
	5				

- Put a few different plants on a table for a small group of children to examine.

- Encourage careful touching and smelling.

- Ask them what they notice about each plant.
  Stimulate or focus observations with questions to draw attention to details.

- Play games where you describe a plant and they have to guess which it is.
  Reverse roles so that they describe and you guess.

- Display plants grouped by pupils' criteria. Put their words on the displays.

Science background

The plant kingdom ranges from microscopic algae to huge trees. Green plants use sunlight to make
food. Ferns are non-flowering plants.

QUESTIONS ⑦ EXTENSIONS ⊖ ASSESSMENT Ⓐ

⑦ What colours can you see?

⑦ Which ones feel smooth?

⑦ What shapes are the leaves?

⊖ What plants can children find on a walk in the park? (Remind children not to touch plants without
asking first.)

Ⓐ Can the children spot different plants in pictures, e.g. of a wood?

Ⓐ What other plants can they tell you about? Do they include big trees and small mosses?

All sorts of plants

Look at some pot plants.

spider plant

cactus.

geranium

Devil's ivy

fern.

Which plants have lots of leaves?
Which plants are spiky?
Choose your favourite plant.
What do you like about it?

SPECTRUM
SCIENCE

Exploring Life and
the Environment
levels 1-3

4   A mossy garden

Making a miniature moist habitat
Providing conditions for small plants to live and grow

Apparatus

PoS	Level	AT1			AT 2
		i	ii	iii	
	1		a		a
2ii	2				
	3				
	4				
	5				

Hand lens
Plastic containers such as ice-cream or margarine tubs
Old aquarium or propagator
Plant spray or dropper
Plastic spoons
Soil or potting compost
Stones
Bark
Moss and other small moisture-loving plants such as small ivies and ferns, snakeskin plant (Fittonia)

- Show children plants in their natural habitat or in one you have created.

- Talk about the conditions and what they think plants need to stay alive and grow.

- Provide apparatus on a table covered with paper or plastic.

- Ask a small group to make a mossy garden in a container. They can spoon in soil or compost so that stones are half buried.

- Talk about where and how to plant the mosses and other plants.

- Encourage them to keep their garden moist but not flooded and to watch their plants.

Science background

Green plants need air, light and water. Some grow best in shady, moist conditions. Mosses are non-flowering green plants. Some grow on dry stones and bricks but most thrive in damp conditions. The particular setting in which plants and animals grow is termed their 'habitat'.

QUESTIONS ⑦ EXTENSIONS ⊖ ASSESSMENT Ⓐ

⑦ What will you do to keep your plants alive?

⑦ What will happen if you forget about them?

⊖ Make a bottle garden.

⊖ Grow seeds under various conditions (see activity 11)

Ⓐ What differences between the plants can children list?

Ⓐ Can they explain what plants need?

A mossy garden

Make a small garden.
Put stones and soil in it.

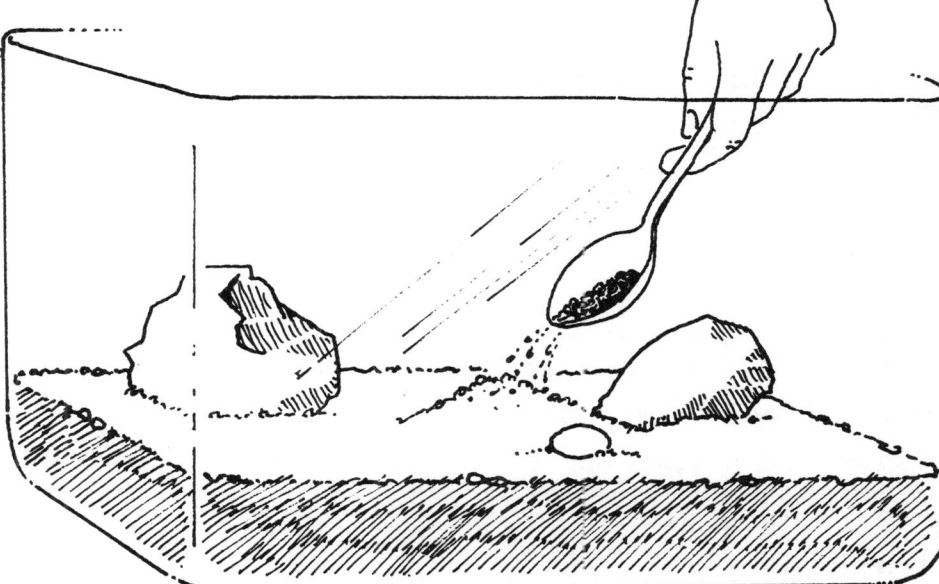

Plant mosses by the stones.
Put in some other plants.

Water them.

SPECTRUM
SCIENCE

*Exploring Life and
the Environment*
levels 1-3

5   Plant eaters

Keeping and feeding small animals
Providing appropriate food plants for small herbivores

PoS	Level	AT1 i	ii	iii	AT 2
2ii	1				
	2	a	b		a
	3				
	4				
	5				

Apparatus

Mossy garden from activity 4 or similar 'home'
Small animals, e.g. snail, slug
Hand lens
Spoon
Gauze or netting or perforated lid with elastic or string to fix it on
Spray or dropper
Supplies of fresh plant material, e.g. bits of lettuce, carrot, cucumber

- Small insects and spiders may have been in the soil or plants when you made the garden. Or they may come in later by air. They could be carefully lifted with a spoon or a dry dropper.

- Encourage close observation and comparison.

- Introduce one or two other plant-eaters like snails. Get children to work out how to keep them in and ask if air has to be let in. You could have various materials available (including netting) to discuss with the children.

- Watch for signs of what the animals eat.

- Ask children to give their animals different foodstuffs (in small quantities) and look after them. Ensure that the animals are treated with care.

Science background

Small plant-eating animals (herbivores) can be kept if they have the right foodplants. Some have specific needs, e.g. many butterfly caterpillars. Some like damp shade, e.g. slugs and snails, and need to be kept moist.

QUESTIONS ② EXTENSIONS ⊖ ASSESSMENT Ⓐ

②   How did any animals get in the garden?

②   Can they live there? What will they need?

⊖   Plan tests to see which foods the animals choose to eat (see activity 6).

⊖   Make suitable homes and provide the right food for other species.

Ⓐ   Can they list the basic needs of small animals, e.g. food, air, water?

Ⓐ   Can they provide for the particular needs of different animals, e.g. shade or shelter for woodlice, damp environment for slugs?

Plant eaters

5

Are there any small animals
in your moss garden?

Put one or two in.
How can you stop them escaping?

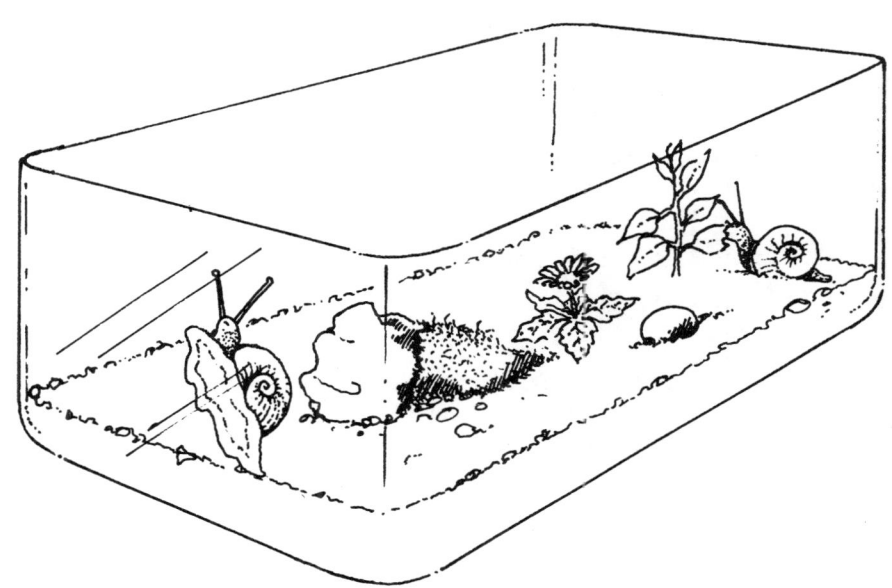

What will they eat?
How much food will you give them?

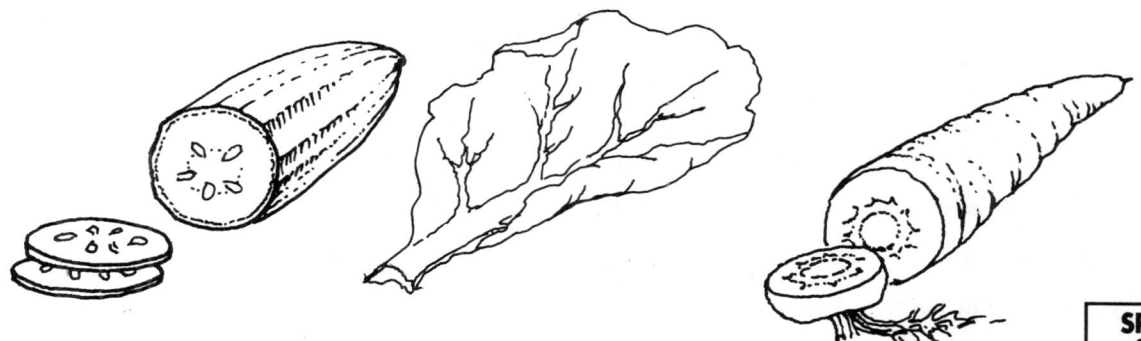

SPECTRUM
SCIENCE

*Exploring Life and
the Environment*
levels 1-3

6 What will it eat?

Investigating food preferences of small animals

Apparatus

Container (ideally a plastic aquarium, otherwise a clear food container or even a tray)
Small animal in 'home' to which it can be returned
Hand lenses

PoS	Level	AT1 i	ii	iii	AT 2
	1				
2iv	2		b		a
	3	a		c	
	4				
	5				

- Slugs or snails are ideal for this. Ensure careful handling and return the animals to their 'home'.

- A group of pupils can discuss what they know and expect about the animal's food preferences. They should plan what foods to provide and how much.

- Encourage close observation of the animal's behaviour before and during eating. Pictures and words can be combined to report the observations. Foodstuffs might be ranked to record results.

- The results may be inconclusive and need checking. The investigation is easy to repeat with slugs. Discussion of the investigation is as important as the results.

Science background

Some animals eat a wide range of foodstuffs; others have very specific needs or preferences. Slugs and snails can be quite selective, as gardeners know! They like lettuce, cabbage, tomatoes, carrots, leaves, flowers and weeds. Variables like amount and moisture need to be controlled to be 'fair' and the results also depend on what counts as 'preferred' food (e.g. the first or the most consumed?)

QUESTIONS ? EXTENSIONS ⊖ ASSESSMENT Ⓐ

(?) What sorts of food do you think your animal will eat?

(?) What will you do if it isn't hungry?

(⊖) Check results with another animal of the same sort. Compare foods that are very similar.

(⊖) What foods do children choose? What use are different foods?

(Ⓐ) Can children suggest ways to improve the investigation?

(Ⓐ) Can they relate the results to what happens in nature?

What will it eat?

Find out what food your animal chooses.

Put different foods in the corners of the container.

Put the animal in the middle.

Which food does it eat?

Watch it closely when it eats.

Was your test fair?

What other foods could you try?

SPECTRUM SCIENCE

Exploring Life and the Environment levels 1-3

7 Plants and sun

Tracing energy from plants

Apparatus

None essential but reference books useful

PoS	Level	AT1			AT 2
		i	ii	iii	
2iv	1		a		
	2				
	3				c
	4				
	5				

- Ideally this should be part of work on local habitats or keeping plants and animals or on food.

- Children may hear and see a lot of information in the media about how trees and other green plants are essential for our survival but they are unlikely to understand their role in trapping energy.

- The layout of the pupil's sheet is designed to emphasise the flow of energy from sunlight through plants to animals. To introduce this flow to young pupils the word food is used at this stage and pupils are asked to list some animals which feed on plants followed by animals which feed on animals.

- As the children use the sheets there should be discussion between them and you in small groups.

- If children's writing is limited, they can draw or sort or select from lists you provide. Draw simple food chains like that down the side of the pupil's sheet.

Science background

Green plants convert energy from sunlight to chemical energy. Some is needed in the plant's living processes and some is stored. Animals cannot do this and depend on plants for their energy source. Some feed directly on plants, others indirectly by eating other animals which have eaten plants.

QUESTIONS ⑦ EXTENSIONS ⊖ ASSESSMENT Ⓐ

⑦ What sorts of food do you eat?

⑦ What are they made of?

⑦ What plants do we grow for food?

⊖ Investigate how light is needed for plant growth (see Activity 11)

Ⓐ Ask children to trace back the source of their food energy.

Ⓐ Ask them what would happen if there were no plants.

Plants and sun

Plants get their food from sunlight.

Some animals eat plants to get their food.
List some animals that eat plants.

_____

_____

_____

_____

_____

_____

_____

Some animals eat other animals to get their food.
List some animals that eat other animals.

_____

_____

_____

_____

_____

Without plants, there would be no food
for animals to eat.
What sorts of plants do you eat?

SPECTRUM SCIENCE

*Exploring Life and
the Environment*
levels 1-3

8   Sensitive animals

Investigating the senses and responses of small animals

Apparatus

Small animal(s) such as slugs or snails (Giant Land Snails are
ideal if available) in a 'home' to which they can be returned
Hand lenses
Water spray
Torch with narrow beam

PoS	Level	AT1 i	ii	iii	AT 2
2i	1				
	2		b		
	3	a			a
	4				
	5				

- This could arise from other activities with animals (e.g. activities 5 and 6) or investigation of human senses in topics like 'Ourselves' or 'Communications'.

- Clarify the terms 'senses' and 'sensitive'.

- Get pairs or groups of children to talk about how they will carry out their investigations. Encourage them to be systematic and to check results.

- Children can record their observations in drawings which can be labelled and sequenced.

- Help them to make considered and cautious generalisations.

- Groups can compare their findings and discuss new and improved investigations.

- Ensure that children treat animals with care and do not overstimulate them (e.g. with sharp or heavy touch). Return them to their 'home' before they overheat or dry out.

Science background

Animals sense changes in their environment (e.g. pressure, movement, sound, light, heat, moisture, taste, smell). They may have special sense organs such as eyes. Snails have two sets of antennae, the lower responding to touch, the upper bearing eyes.
Animals respond to information from their senses, e.g. by moving.

QUESTIONS ⑦ EXTENSIONS ⊖ ASSESSMENT Ⓐ

⑦ What can you do to the animal that will not harm it? How gentle can you be?

⑦ How will you know if it feels anything?

⊖ What senses do we use and how do we take care of sense organs like eyes and ears?

⊖ Explore responses of other animals – e.g. fish in a tank can be fed, stimulated by noise or light.

Ⓐ Are children carrying out their investigations carefully and checking results?

Ⓐ Can they interpret what they observe and suggest further tests?

Sensitive animals

What can your animal feel?

How can you find out without harming it?

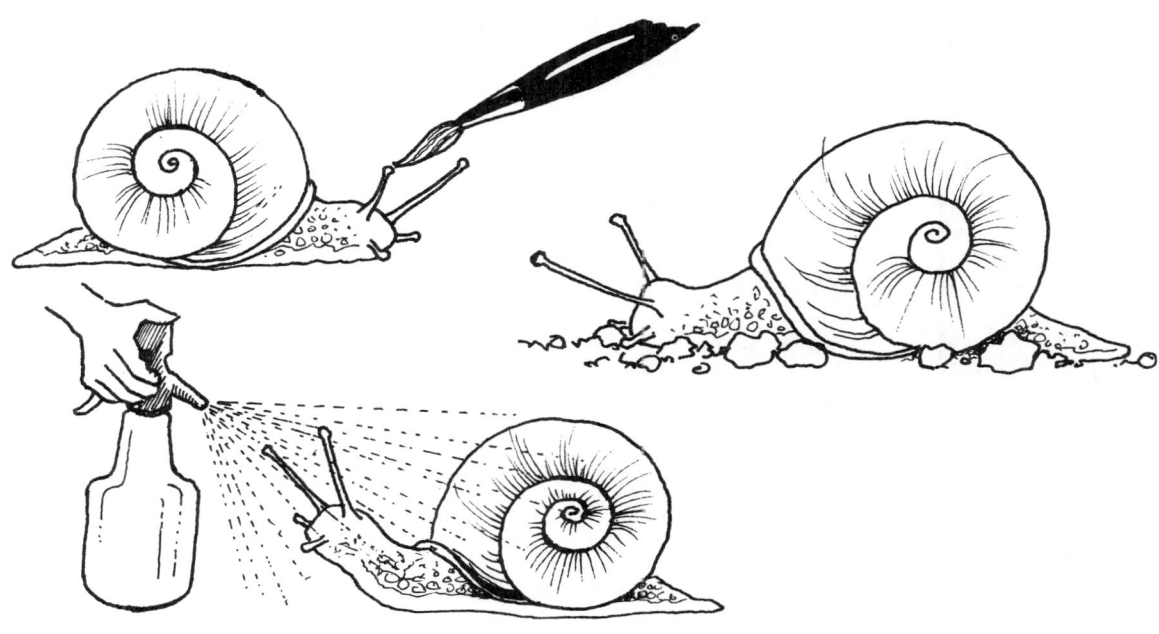

Where is it most sensitive?

What does it do when it feels something?

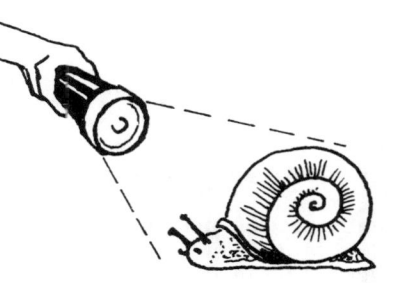

Find out if it can hear and see.

SPECTRUM
SCIENCE

*Exploring Life and
the Environment*
levels 1-3

9 Flowers, fruits, seeds

Observing seeds in fruits and flowers
Matching seeds to fruits, flowers and plants

Apparatus

Fruits and flowers with visible seeds (different stages and types
in season, including wild plants as well as cultivated ones)
Hand lens
Radish seeds – extension activities

PoS	Level	AT1 i	ii	iii	AT 2
2i	1				
	2		b		b
	3	a			
	4				
	5				

- Avoid poisonous seeds and fruits (e.g. laburnum, nightshade, spindle tree, yew). Teach children that some are unsafe to eat and touch. If possible provide some fruits that are still attached to the plant or have remnants of the plant on them. Have pictures of the plants they come from.

- Examine flowers, fruits and seeds at different stages from formation to dispersal. Fruit bushes, shrubs and trees, garden flowers and weeds (such as rose-bay willow herb) can all be useful.

- Observational drawing of fruits is common in schools. Here it is used to focus observation on seeds and their development by comparing seeds in different fruits and at different stages. Draw attention to any evidence that the fruit formed from a flower.

Science background

Flowers form seeds which are often carried in fruits. Children's ideas of 'fruit' may be restricted to sweet, edible ones that can be bought in greengrocers. They may not learn the relationships between flowers, fruits, seeds and plant reproduction from isolated experiences.

QUESTIONS ⑦ EXTENSIONS ⊖ ASSESSMENT Ⓐ

⑦ Where are the seeds? How many are there?

⑦ How do they feel? What do they look like?

⊖ Grow plants from seed (see activities 10 and 11). Try different varieties of radish for quick results.
Draw cartoon strips to show how flowers form and produce seeds which are dispersed in a plant they study.

Ⓐ Can children find seeds in unfamiliar plants?

Ⓐ Can they suggest ways to identify seeds?

Flowers, fruits, seeds

Find the seeds in a fruit.

Draw the fruit to show the seeds.

Look at some
different fruits.

Mix up some of
their seeds.

Can you sort out
which seeds belong
to which fruit?

SPECTRUM
SCIENCE

*Exploring Life and
the Environment*
levels 1-3

10   Seed sorts

Observing seeds
Matching seeds to the plants they grow into
Germinating seeds

Apparatus

Seeds in packets (a selection of fast growing sorts such as
mustard and cress, sprouting beans, radish, lettuce)
Trays
Compost or soil
Hand lens

PoS	Level	AT1 i	ii	iii	AT 2
	1				
2i	2		b		b
	3				
	4				
	5				

- Avoid poisonous seeds and teach children to beware packets that have treated seeds as they can be poisonous. Avoid pelleted seeds as they will be confusing.

- Encourage close observation of seeds and compare the small differences between seeds with the larger differences between plants shown on packet illustrations.

- Sprouting seeds can be germinated rapidly on moist blotting paper or in jars and their growth recorded while other seeds grow in compost. Check seed packets for suitable times and conditions.

- Organise groups to sow different trays. Involve the class in watching the growth by displaying the trays with a diary of the drawings they make.

- Look out for signs that show what the plant will eventually be.

Science background

Seeds come from flowers and some germinate and grow into specific plants which produce more of the same seeds. Commercially produced seeds have a higher chance of germinating than those in the wild. When they first appear, seedlings look very similar.

QUESTIONS ⑦ EXTENSIONS ⊖ ASSESSMENT Ⓐ

⑦ Are the seeds all the same size?

⑦ What's different about them?

⑦ If we mixed the seeds up could you put them into the right packets?

⊖ Grow a mixture of seeds together and spot what sorts of plants develop.

⊖ Growing seeds should stimulate other investigations (see activities 11 and 16). Salad plants can be eaten.

Ⓐ Can children carry out and record the investigation systematically?

Seed sorts

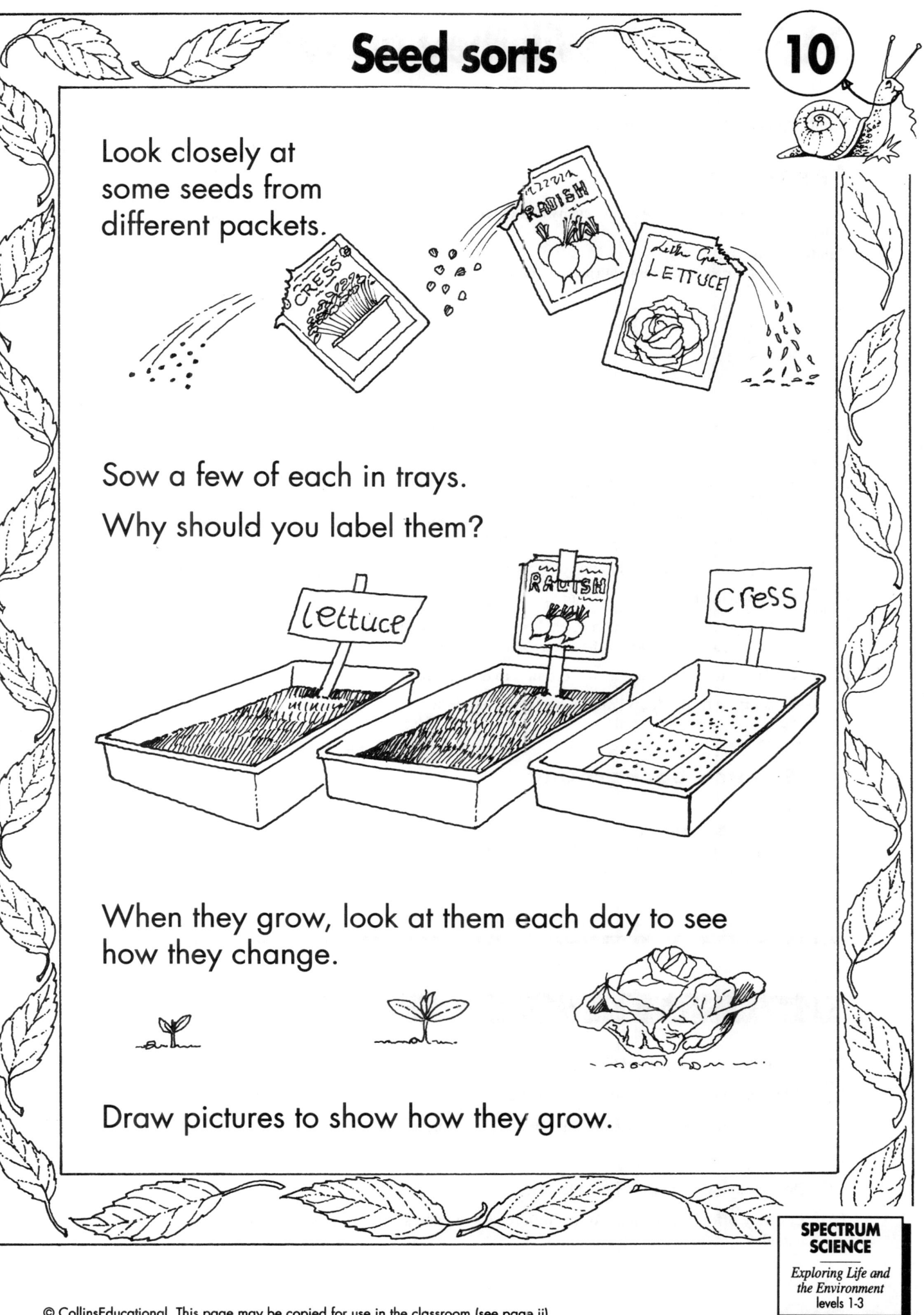

Look closely at some seeds from different packets.

Sow a few of each in trays.

Why should you label them?

When they grow, look at them each day to see how they change.

Draw pictures to show how they grow.

SPECTRUM SCIENCE

Exploring Life and the Environment levels 1-3

11 Will they grow?

Exploring conditions needed for seedlings to grow

PoS	Level	AT1 i	AT1 ii	AT1 iii	AT 2
2i	1				
	2		b		
	3	a			c
	4				
	5				

Apparatus

Seedlings or seeds which will grow easily and quickly, e.g.
radishes
Small trays or containers
Growing medium such as multi-purpose compost

- Grow seeds or get seedlings in small trays. Use seeds which have just been germinated by pupils or provide identical trays of small seedlings.
  Show children some which have grown well, others that are pale and spindly, some which have wilted. Discuss what might affect their growth.

- Grow some in the light and some in the dark. Ensure they are equally warm and moist.

- Help children to draw their predictions and what actually happens on a large chart.

- Compare growth in warm v. cold, wet v. dry circumstances but beware confusing children with too many variables. Ensure the other conditions are controlled. (Note links with activities 4 and 10.)

- The activity provides an opportunity to design propagators.

- Story to read: *Meg's Garden* by Jan Pienkowski.

Science background

Seeds need moisture and suitable temperatures to germinate - read the packets for particular requirements. To grow successfully, seedlings need water, air, sufficient light and warmth. Minerals are absorbed by water from the soil or supplied by liquid fertiliser.

QUESTIONS ② EXTENSIONS ⊖ ASSESSMENT Ⓐ

(?) What do you notice about these plants?

(?) What do you think has made them grow like that?

⊖ How do pupils think they could investigate plants' needs for water?

⊖ What else might they test?

Ⓐ Do they know how to keep pot plants alive?

Ⓐ Can they offer explanations for the differences in the way plants are growing in contrasting conditions outside?

Will they grow?

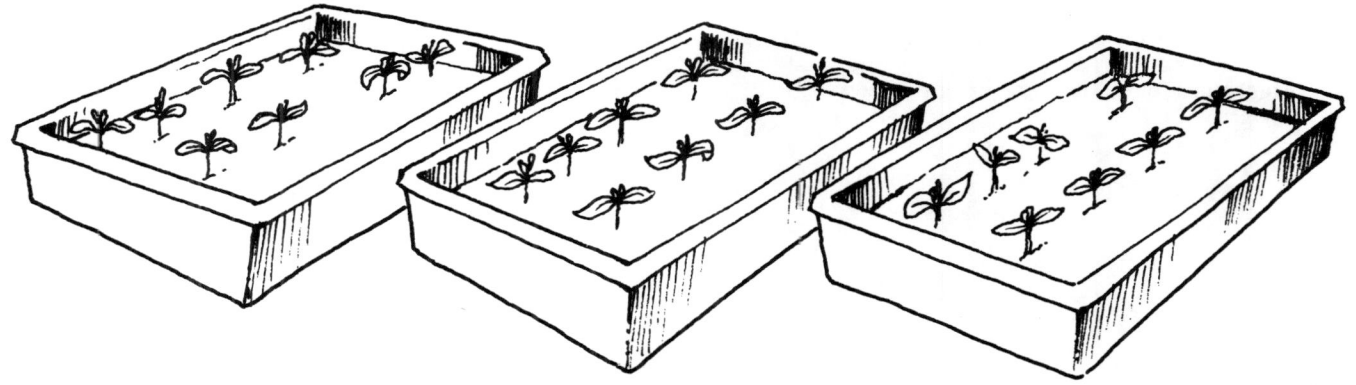

These small plants have started to grow.
What do you think they need?

Put one tray somewhere light.
Put another in the dark.

Put some in a warm place and some
where it is cold.

What will happen if you do not water all
your plants?

SPECTRUM SCIENCE

Exploring Life and the Environment
levels 1-3

12   Spot the differences

Observing differences and similarities between children

Apparatus

Large mirror for use by pairs of children

Magazines for cutting up – extension activity

PoS	Level	AT1			AT 2
		i	ii	iii	
2ii	1		a		
	2				b
	3				
	4				
	5				

- The starter activity of spotting differences between children will probably be familiar to them. At first, accept any accurate observations. Then help children identify relevant physical variations rather than transient features like clothes or hair styles.

- Encourage observations of similarities as well as differences in other class activities as well. In this case children can begin to see how small individual variations are when compared to the common characteristics of the human species.

- Some children may be able to list their observations as they work in pairs. With the whole class, group them in various ways (e.g. by eye colour). Then get them to talk about it and use mapping and set diagrams.

- Bear in mind the school's policies for exploring differences of colour and race, family likenesses, and any handicaps or features such as obesity.

Science background

Most differences pupils see will be minor and not significant. However they introduce the idea of variation within a species. Individuals of any species vary. Some variations are inherited. They can be significant for survival and hence for evolution by selection, e.g. colouring which camouflages and so reduces the chances of being eaten.

QUESTIONS ⑦ EXTENSIONS ⊖ ASSESSMENT Ⓐ

⑦ Tell me what your partner looks like.

⑦ Can you describe to me what you look like?

⊖ Make up identikit pictures from features cut out of colour magazines.

⊖ Compare individuals of another available species (e.g. sparrows in the yard, clover as you seek one with 4 leaves).

Ⓐ Can a child list relevant observations?

Ⓐ Ask a child to describe another. Who can identify them from the description?

Spot the differences

What differences can you spot between these two children?

Find a friend.

What things about you are the same?

SPECTRUM
SCIENCE

Exploring Life and the Environment
levels 1-3

13 What size?

Exploring individual differences by measuring and comparing feet and heads

Apparatus

Large pieces of thin card or thick paper (the reverse side of paper previously used will do)
Scissors

Shoe boxes
Talcum powder, tray, black paper } extension activities

PoS	Level	AT1 i	ii	iii	AT 2
	1		a		a
2ii	2				
	3				
	4				
	5				

- This could be part of a topic on 'Ourselves' or maths work. It could be stimulated by a visit to a shoe shop and/or setting up a shoe shop play area. Confusion over shoes or clothes on a wet day or after PE could be an opportunity! Stress the importance of wearing shoes of the right size.

- Promote careful, consistent drawing (e.g. is everybody's foot in the same position? Which foot will you use?)

- Direct measurement (e.g. cut a paper strip to the length), non-standard or standard units can be used according to children's level of maths. Some may appreciate that area could be estimated.

- Rank ordering of the children's foot silhouettes is the simplest record. Long thin and short wide feet may create a need for other ways of recording such as charts and simple graphs.

- Hands and gloves can be compared by similar methods. More details can be recorded than with feet! Hand and footprints can be made using talcum powder and black paper.

Science background

Children differ in their size and rate of development. Their feet and hands may show inherited variations of size and shape. Fingerprints are good examples of individual differences.

QUESTIONS ⊙ EXTENSIONS ⊖ ASSESSMENT Ⓐ

⊙ Do people with big feet have big hands?

⊙ What would you measure before making a pair of mittens?

⊖ Make party hats and measure heads so that they fit – but beware sensitivity or teasing about big heads.

⊖ Design and make a foot-measuring device (e.g. using a shoe box).

⊖ Try recording fingerprints and measuring fingers (see activity 14).

Ⓐ Do children measure carefully and consistently?

What size?

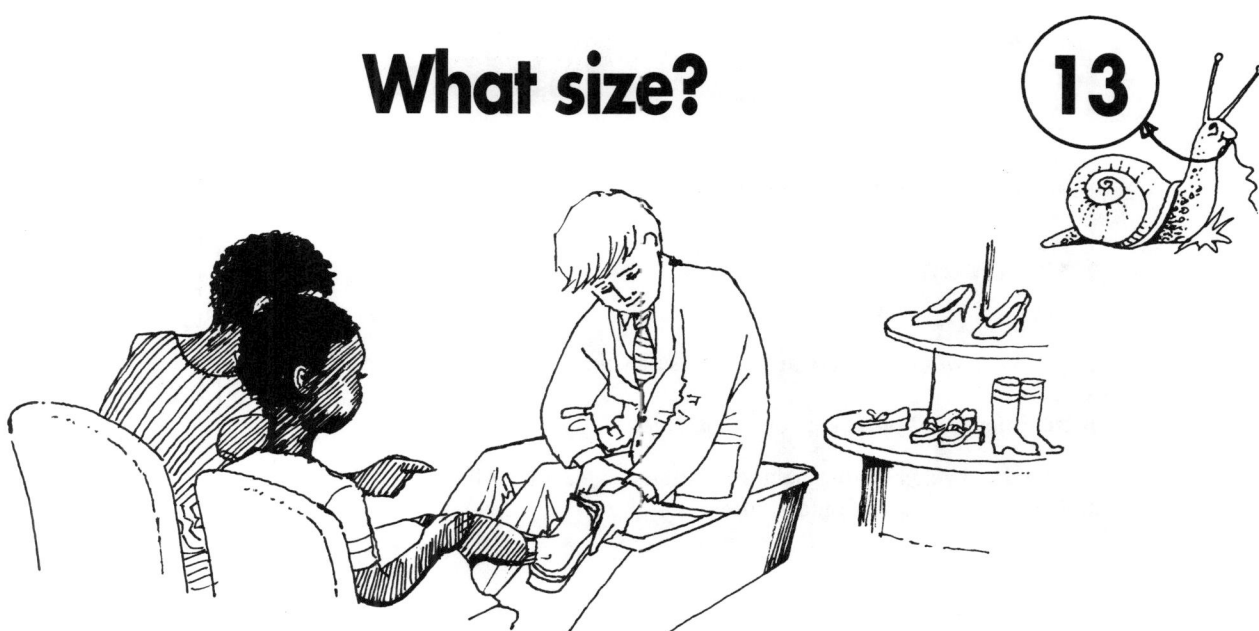

Why is the man measuring the girl's foot?

Find out how big your feet are.

Draw round one
and cut out
the shape.

How long is it? ....

How wide is it? ....

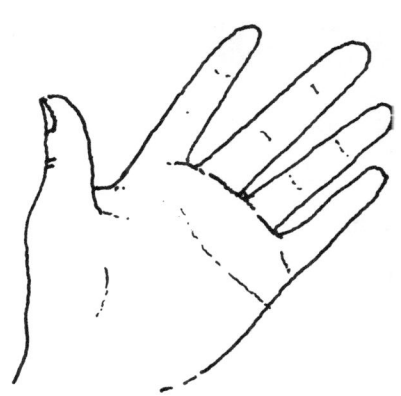

How big are
your hands?

SPECTRUM
SCIENCE

Exploring Life and
the Environment
levels 1-3

14   Fingers

Exploring individual differences in fingers

Apparatus

Tray
Thread and lots of beads (choose sizes to suit your pupils'
dexterity)
1 minute timer (sand or tocker) or a stop clock

Elastic bands, springs, spring balance, weight scale, rubber balls,
plasticine or clay – extension activities

PoS	Level	AT1			AT 2
		i	ii	iii	
	1				a
2ii	2				
	3	a	b	c	
	4				
	5				

- Give a small group of children the apparatus on a tray. Ask them to work on the tray so that beads do not roll away.

- Encourage fair testing and checking of results. Give help with recording results if necessary.

- Other ideas for testing should be discussed to see if they are safe and feasible. Tests of finger strength may need supervision. Pulling and pushing might be difficult to test accurately.

- These activities test dexterity as well as size and strength to give different children opportunities to do well.

Science background

Children's sense of touch, size of bones, strength, dexterity and hand-eye co-ordination vary between individuals. These variations will reflect inherited differences, environmental influences and teaching of skills. Some children may have particular attributes (e.g. double-jointedness).

QUESTIONS ⑦ EXTENSIONS ⊖ ASSESSMENT Ⓐ

⑦ When do you need small, nimble fingers?

⑦ When are big, strong fingers useful?

⑦ How are your fingers different from your thumb?

⊖ List and demonstrate things children can do with their fingers.

⊖ Devise tests of finger strength using springs or elastic bands, squeezy balls, clay, plasticine.

Ⓐ Can children see any patterns in their results?

Fingers

14

Look at each others' hands.
How are they different?

Try these finger tests.

Can you do this?

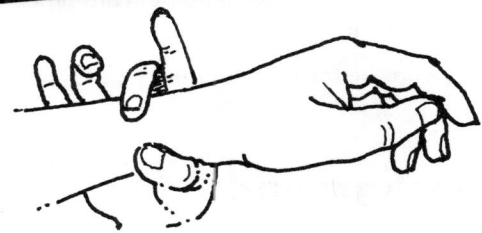

Now try it with your friend's wrist.

How many beads can
each of you hold in one
hand?

How many can you thread
in one minute?

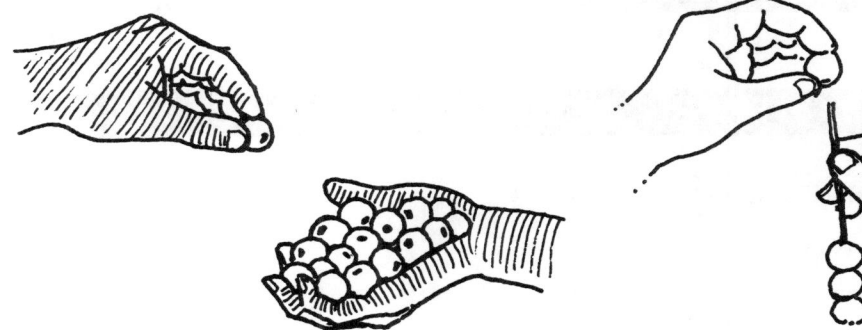

Can you think of any other ways to test fingers?

SPECTRUM
SCIENCE

*Exploring Life and
the Environment*
levels 1-3

15   Comparing plants

Comparing, describing and drawing a variety of plants

Apparatus

Variety of plants as available (e.g. bedding plants such as
pansies and lobelia, specimens in the garden or lawn such as
dandelions and daisies)
Seed packets, plant labels, garden catalogues for pictures and
concise descriptions of plants
Containers and soil or compost
Hand lens

PoS	Level	AT1 i	AT1 ii	AT1 iii	AT 2
	1				
2ii	2		b		b
	3				
	4				
	5				

- Give children a few contrasting plants or pictures to compare.

- Provide a few labels or packets with descriptions they can match to the specimens or pictures.

- Encourage talk about distinctive features.

- Organise them to make large labels on which they can illustrate and describe different plants. The labels could be pasted on to stiff card, sealed and stuck on a stick.

- Encourage concise, accurate descriptions. Word processing would be useful. The labels could be made for seeds and plants grown in other activities (e.g. 4, 10 and 11).

- Give children a purpose for growing things e.g. planning a plant sale, making a patchwork garden.

Science background

Different sorts of living things are classified into groups largely on the basis of their structure. At this level children can begin to recognise some characteristics of groups and distinguish varieties or species by appearance. Flowering plants can be distinguished by features such as the shape, size and arrangement of leaves (see activity 3); their habit (e.g. low and creeping); stems and stalk; and, if in flower, by colour, number and arrangement of petals.

QUESTIONS ⑦ EXTENSIONS ⊖ ASSESSMENT Ⓐ

⑦ How big is the plant? Is it tall?

⑦ What are the leaves like?

⑦ Does it have flowers?

⊖ Visit a garden centre and find out how they group and list plants.

⊖ Compile a database of plants (e.g. using 'Noticeboard').

Ⓐ Play a game of 20 questions where children have to identify a plant you think of. Reverse roles.

Comparing plants

15

Look at two plants.

How are they different?

What is the same about them?

How do you know what these plants will look like?

Make labels that describe your plants.

Draw a picture to show what each sort of plant looks like.

SPECTRUM
SCIENCE

*Exploring Life and
the Environment*
levels 1-3

16   Sorting leaves

Sorting leaves by observed similarities and differences

Apparatus

A variety of leaves (fallen leaves from trees in autumn, and/or other plants)
Hand lenses
Large scrap paper, hoops or string will be useful but not essential

Database such as *DIY database*, *Grass*, *Junior Find*
Well-illustrated books such as Oxford Clue Books (OUP) and
Eyewitness Guide – *Plant* (Dorling Kindersley)

PoS	Level	AT1			AT 2
		i	ii	iii	
	1				
2ii	2		b		b
	3				
	4				
	5				

△ • Ideally pupils should collect their own leaves (avoid Yew). If you provide them, mix a few contrasting sorts. Later add others to extend the task or to introduce certain features, such as hairs or veins or serrated edges.

• Build on previous sorting work and use of sets. Let children sort by whatever features they choose at first. Then draw attention to things they may not notice, for instance the arrangement of leaves on stems.

• Encourage naming of parts and recognition of common features as well as differences.

📖 • Rubbings draw attention to details and make a record which can be developed with drawings, pressing and preserving leaves.

Science background

Leaves on trees and other plants may occur singly or grouped on a stem. Compound leaves are divided into several leaflets; simple leaves are not. The species, or larger group, to which a plant belongs can often be identified from its leaves.

QUESTIONS ⑦ EXTENSIONS ⊖ ASSESSMENT Ⓐ

⑦ What is the same about these two leaves?

⑦ How many differences can you see between them?

⑦ Which ones do you think go together?

⑦ How is this group different from that one?

⊖ Use a database on the computer to sort the leaves.

⊖ Identify leaves from pictures in books.

Ⓐ Do children identify similarities as well as differences?

Sorting leaves

16

Look closely at a collection of leaves.

In what ways are they all the same?
What differences can you find between leaves?

Sort them into groups.

Here is one way you could try.

Here is another.

How else can you sort them?

SPECTRUM SCIENCE

Exploring Life and the Environment
levels 1-3

17   **Food**

Distinguishing food and non-food
Identifying food from plants and animals

Apparatus

None

PoS	Level	AT1			AT 2
		i	ii	iii	
	1		a		
2i	2				
	3				a
	4				
	5				

- Talk about the sorts of food the children eat.

- Mention the dangers of eating things which might be poisonous like some berries, laburnum and lupin seeds.

- Talk about vegans who only eat food from plants and vegetarians who do not eat meat or fish.

- When children have filled in the table with the foods in the pictures, encourage them to extend it with more foods. You could make a larger version for display with children's pictures glued on.

Science background

People get food from both plants and animals. Vegetarians do not eat animals for a variety of reasons. All plants trap energy from the Sun in their leaves. Plants provide rich sources of stored energy. All animals, including people, ultimately rely on plants for their energy.

QUESTIONS ⑦ EXTENSIONS ⊖ ASSESSMENT Ⓐ

⑦   What is your favourite food?

⑦   Which foods do you think give you energy?

⑦   Which sort of food comes from cows?

⊖   Bring in some whole grains of wheat. Grind it into flour using stones. Many children will not know that bread is made from special grass seed (wheat).

Ⓐ   Can the children describe meals which include both vegetables and meat?

Food

17

Circle all the things you could eat.   Put them in this table.

Food			
from animals		from plants	

Add more foods.

SPECTRUM SCIENCE

Exploring Life and the Environment levels 1-3

18 Healthy days

Identifying activities contributing to children's safety and
healthy development
Examining patterns of daily activity

Apparatus

Paper and card to make big drawings for a zig-zag book or strip
cartoon

PoS	Level	AT1			AT 2
		i	ii	iii	
	1		a		
2i	2				a
	3				
	4				
	5				

- This activity could follow from group or class discussion in the course of health education or topics on 'Ourselves' or 'Time'.

- Use large pictures as prompts or guide children's descriptions of their day to focus the discussion.

- Help small groups or individuals draw their own ideas. Encourage talk about what they need to grow safe and healthy and how their own activities help. If necessary, add words to their drawings and help them arrange them in a sequence.

- Introduce ideas which have wider significance for health and safety (use of movement and senses to be safe on roads, need for exercise and rest, hygiene, balanced diet and water).

Science background

Like other animals the young human being's safe and healthy development depends on suitable supplies of food and water, using their sensory and motor systems, avoiding hazards. People can take more informed, active steps than other animals.

QUESTIONS ⑦ EXTENSIONS ⊖ ASSESSMENT Ⓐ

⑦ Why do you think you need food? What sorts are good for you?

⑦ When do you take exercise/rest?

⑦ What else should you do each day?

⊖ Make posters promoting safe behaviour, healthy living. Look at adverts children encounter.

⊖ Discuss threats to health and safety. Begin from those most relevant to your pupils but be tactful.

Ⓐ Do children know why they need to sleep, keep clean, exercise?

Healthy days

18

Talk about what you do each day to keep safe and healthy.

sleeping

exercise

crossing road carefully

Draw pictures of ways you keep yourself healthy.

brushing teeth

eating fruit

When do you do each of them?
Put your pictures in order to make the story of a healthy day.

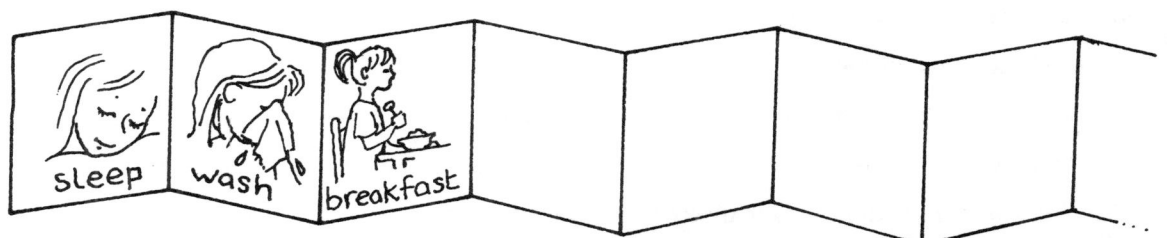

sleep wash breakfast

SPECTRUM SCIENCE

Exploring Life and the Environment
levels 1-3

19 Growing older

Matching people to photographs of their younger selves
Identifying changes which occur as humans grow older

Apparatus

Photographs of the children as babies
Photos of themselves and adults they know at various ages

PoS	Level	AT1			AT 2
		i	ii	iii	
	1				
2i	2				
	3		b		a
	4				
	5				

- This might be part of a topic on 'Ourselves' or 'Changes' and link with historical work. Extend the familiar activity of displaying family photos and identifying babies to focus attention on changes that occur as humans grow. Be cautious and tactful about family likenesses.

- After initial observations explore the changes which are developmental features rather than incidentals.

- Relative sizes of heads and limbs can be compared as well as overall height. Children of different ages can be measured or graphed directly by standing them against a board or paper pinned on the wall.

- Illustrate growing competence and independence through childhood and adolescence with reference to siblings. Discuss what is learned and what develops without teaching.

- Help children to chart and discuss their physical development, abilities and needs. Display these as a strip on the wall or in a zig-zag book.

Science background

Compared with other animals, humans have an extended childhood during which they learn a lot. Physical and mental development follows a predictable sequence but individual differences and environmental influences affect how each child develops.

QUESTIONS ⑦ EXTENSIONS ⊖ ASSESSMENT Ⓐ

⑦ How many ways have you changed since this photo?

⑦ How much have you grown?

⊖ Ask a parent to bring in a baby and a toddler (you may want them at different times!)

⊖ Ask a senior citizen to talk with children about her life and show them pictures of herself.

Ⓐ What physical changes from baby to their present age can children list?

Ⓐ Can they identify similarities and differences with growth of another mammal (e.g. a pet)?

Growing older

19

Look closely at a baby photo
of someone in the class.

How have they changed since the photo was taken?

Use photos or drawings to show how someone
changes as they grow up.

taller
no nappies
teeth
feeds himself
talks

baby

starting school.

Put words between each picture to say what changes.

SPECTRUM
SCIENCE

*Exploring Life and
the Environment*
levels 1-3

20　Dying Out

Drawing endangered and extinct species

Apparatus

Reference books and pictures of animals, including extinct species

PoS	Level	AT1			AT 2
		i	ii	iii	
	1				
2ii	2				
	3				b
	4				
	5				

- Any work on extinction will require suitable secondary sources of information. Museum visits would enrich the topic. Children are made aware of endangered species and the campaigns to save them through the media. These could be a starting point.

- Discuss with children what threatens the survival of the species they are drawing.

- Draw their attention to illustrations of animals which are extinct. Help them sort out those which disappeared before humans appeared from later ones where they could include people in their pictures.

- Posters can be made and displayed or small pictures compiled into a book or made into postcards or packs of cards for later use. Children could produce symbols and slogans as well as pictures.

Science background

Many plant and animal species are threatened with extinction. The loss of habitats, pollution and climate change resulting from human activity will threaten more in children's lifetimes. In the recent past, species such as the dodo became extinct. Prehistoric animals like the woolly mammoth existed at the same time as early humans. Dinosaurs died out long before.

QUESTIONS ② EXTENSIONS ⊖ ASSESSMENT Ⓐ

- ② Which animals have you heard about that may not survive?
- ② Do you know any sorts of animals that used to live but do not live nowadays?
- ② Were there people living at the same time as ...?
- ⊖ Make a time line, arranging animals on it to show when they died out.
- ⊖ Put pictures in sets, add backgrounds and, where appropriate, people.
- Ⓐ Can children identify animals that died out in a historical time?

Dying out

20

Draw some posters about animals that are in danger of dying out.

Make some other posters about animals that have already died out.

WHAT HAPPENED TO THE

WOOLLY MAMMOTHS?

DON'T BE A DINOSAUR

Which animals died so long ago that nobody ever saw them alive?

SPECTRUM SCIENCE

Exploring Life and the Environment levels 1-3

Habitats

Matching species to habitats

Apparatus

None but it would be useful to have reference books with details of specific habitats, such as ponds or fields or woods for extension activities

PoS	Level	AT1			AT 2
		i	ii	iii	
2iii	1		a		
	2				c
	3				
	4				
	5				

- This activity is best done as part of a study of a local habitat. If your school is not near varied habitats, the area for study can be as small as a little patch of soil, the area under stones or part of a wall.

- The idea that animals live in places which meet their particular needs is probably quite easy for children to grasp. Although they will not expect a tadpole to live on a lawn, they may not realise how some animals can only live in very restricted habitats and others are more able to survive in a variety of places. Plants' specific needs and the habitats that match them may be less obvious. This can be explored in associated or earlier work making homes for animals and plants (see activity 4).

- Matching by drawing lines on the pupil's sheet can be repeated with drawings the children make. Pictures of habitats can be populated by their drawings or cutouts from magazines. Make and display large friezes or 3-D models.

Science background

The type of environment in which a plant or animal is found is called its habitat. Different plants and animals have particular needs which limit the environments where they can thrive. Examples of the environmental conditions that might determine whether they live in a specific habitat include light levels, temperature, moisture, the presence of suitable food plants, competition for food from other animals. The different sorts of plants and animals which populate a particular habitat are called a community.

QUESTIONS ☺ EXTENSIONS ⊖ ASSESSMENT Ⓐ

(?) What animals do you know that live in ponds? (Whichever habitat your pupils are studying)

(?) Do any plants grow in ponds and streams?

(?) What do you think could not live in or by a pond?

(→) Create a small habitat for a particular animal - for instance a wormery for earthworms, a home for woodlice.

(→) Compare two contrasting places to see what lives in each.

(Ⓐ) Can children match animals and plants to the right habitat?

(Ⓐ) Can they draw another sort of habitat which they have met and put appropriate animals and/or plants in it?

Habitats

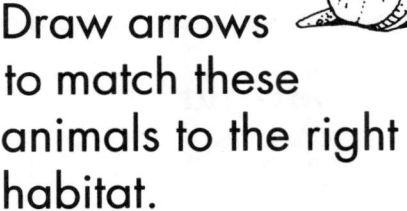

21

The place where an animal or plant lives is called its habitat.

Here are two different habitats:

Draw arrows to match these animals to the right habitat.

Draw a picture of another sort of habitat.
Put in some animals and plants that can live there.

SPECTRUM
SCIENCE

Exploring Life and the Environment
levels 1-3

22   **Waste**

Talking about things which we use, then throw away
Personal responsibility for proper disposal

Apparatus

Sweet wrappers
Crisp bags
Pop bottles and cans
Orange peel
Any other child-used wrappers or containers

PoS	Level	AT1			AT 2
		i	ii	iii	
2iii	1		a		
	2				d
	3				
	4				
	5				

- Make a small collection of wrappers likely to be used by children. Avoid sharp edges.

- Talk about each in turn. This discussion could take place in small or large groups.

- Children could make a waste collage. Make a collection of packages, sweet wrappers. Write short captions using the children's words.

Science background

Packaging uses resources. People are responsible for their own waste. All natural materials such as apple peel and orange peel are readily biodegradable, although orange peel takes longer than you might think. Paper wrapping decays rapidly also. Most metal waste is sorted and recycled. Plastics are usually too complex to recycle but they are virtually indestructible.

QUESTIONS ⑦ EXTENSIONS ⊖ ASSESSMENT Ⓐ

⑦ What was this (item) used for?

⑦ Which of these things are often left as litter?

⑦ Are any of the objects sharp or dangerous?

⊖ Talk about the waste water we put down drains.

Ⓐ Can each child tell you about things they throw away.

Waste

What was inside these wrappers?

22

Which of them do you use?

Where do you put the wrappers when you have finished?

SPECTRUM SCIENCE

Exploring Life and the Environment
levels 1-3

23   Rubbish collection

Sorting household waste. Looking at a variety of containers

Apparatus

About 10-15 pieces of safe and clean household rubbish
including: cans, plastic containers, glass jars, paper products and
wrapping of all kinds
PE hoops
Pieces of card for labels

PoS	Level	AT1			AT 2
		i	ii	iii	
2iv	1		a		
	2				d
	3				
	4				
	5				

* Bring in a range of rubbish from home. You could ask the children, but they may bring unsuitable things.

* The children can work in small groups on the floor if no table space is available.

* Encourage the children to group the rubbish in different ways, e.g. things which hold liquid, see-through things, things with corners, coloured things.

* Ask the children to draw all the objects from one group. Write down their words in a brief caption.

Science background

The majority of household waste is packaging. Liquids are kept in a variety of impermeable materials: plastics; aluminium and steel; glass and waxed paper.

QUESTIONS ② EXTENSIONS ⊖ ASSESSMENT Ⓐ

② Which containers are plastic?

② Which containers feel warm/cold to touch?

② Which packages have several layers?

⊖ Test the containers to find out how strong they are.

Ⓐ Can the pupils tell you about other things which are thrown away?

23

Rubbish collection

These are some of the things we throw away.

Put them in groups.
Use the hoops to help.

Explain to other people why you have put things in a group.

SPECTRUM SCIENCE

Exploring Life and the Environment
levels 1-3

24 Rotting food

Looking at the process of decay in waste food
Recording in the form of a pictorial diary

PoS	Level	AT1			AT 2
		i	ii	iii	
	1				
2iv	2		b		d
	3	a		d	
	4				
	5				

Apparatus

Small pieces of waste food, e.g. carrot, apple, bread, orange
peel, stale pastry, stale cake, cheese
Clear plastic containers with lids (glass jam jars will do)
Magnifying glasses
Magnifying boxes (e.g. magnispectors)

- Talk about what happens to food when it is left. Introduce the word 'mouldy'. Talk about keeping food fresh and healthy.

- Put the foods on a plate for the children to look at, handle and talk about.

- Do not let children handle the mouldy foods. Put them in separate containers with lids. Look at them every three or four days and talk about the changes.

- Fold A4 or A3 paper in four. Ask pupils to draw the food as it changes. The fourth picture should be done about a fortnight after the start of the activity.

Science background

Decay in food takes place when moulds and bacteria grow and break down the food. Some produce harmful toxins so keep the lid on. If the food and jars were sterile and airtight, rotting would not take place.

QUESTIONS ⑦ EXTENSIONS ⊖ ASSESSMENT Ⓐ

⑦ Which foods seem to dry out first?

⑦ Did the cut surfaces change before the peel, e.g. apple?

⑦ What do they smell like? (No touching though once rotting has begun.)

⊖ Observe more closely with magnifying glasses.

Ⓐ Can the children tell you what happened to the waste food?

Rotting food

Look at some pieces of waste food.

apple

pastry

cheese

cake

carrot

orange peel

Which foods do you think will go mouldy quickly?

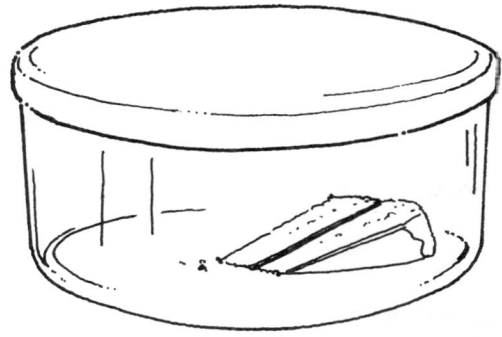

Put them in
separate jars.

Draw what each looks like.

Watch them for about two weeks.

Make drawings to show how they change.

What do you think caused the changes?

SPECTRUM SCIENCE

*Exploring Life and
the Environment*
levels 1-3

25 Buried waste

Looking at the way a variety of waste materials change when buried in soil

Apparatus

Collection of small pieces of waste material such as paper of different kinds:
plastic (e.g. bottle top)
metal (e.g. bottle top)
wood (e.g. piece of lolly stick)
apple peel
orange peel
ice cream container (or similar)
soil
labels

PoS	Level	AT1 i	AT1 ii	AT1 iii	AT 2
2iv	1				
	2		b		d
	3				
	4				
	5				

- Talk about what happens to materials when they are thrown away. Discuss burial in soil.

- Bury the samples in garden soil using a spoon. Remember to keep some to compare with the buried ones.

- Ask children to think of a way to mark what is buried where. Water the soil sparingly.

- Carefully dig up the objects each week or tip them on to a plastic sheet. Re-bury and re-mark each object. Children should wash their hands afterwards.

- Keep a class diary with contributions from different children showing the progress of the experiment.

Science background

Much waste is buried in landfill sites. Some materials such as plastics are very resistant to change. Paper on the other hand is rapidly broken down by soil bacteria and mould.

QUESTIONS ⑦ EXTENSIONS ⊖ ASSESSMENT Ⓐ

⑦ Which things change colour when they are buried?

⑦ Which hardly change at all?

⑦ Why do you think things rot better when they are buried in the soil?

⊖ Look at a garden compost heap.

⊖ Visit a landfill site if the manager agrees.

Ⓐ Do the children notice that only some materials decay quickly?

Buried waste

25

Bury some waste things in soil.

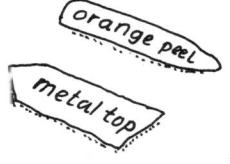

Look at them a week later.
Have they changed?

Put them back.
Look again next week.

SPECTRUM
SCIENCE

*Exploring Life and
the Environment*
levels 1-3

26   Metal decay

Investigating change in non-biological materials
Designing simple investigations

Apparatus

Several iron nails
Staples
Drawing pins
Coins
Cutlery (stainless steel)

PoS	Level	AT1			AT 3
		i	ii	iii	
	1				
3i	2				
	3	a	c	c	a
	4				
	5				

- ⚠ ● Bring in a very rusty object (beware sharp edges).
  What do the children think rust is?
  Get them to describe it and scrape off the coating.

- ● Ask the children if they have noticed rusty objects.

- ● Look at rusty things around the school and draw the children's attention to what they are made from.

- ● Give the children several shiny nails to begin with.

- ● Start the activity by getting children to draw what they think will happen to things left in the rain.

- ● Draw pictures to record the progress of the rusting experiments.

Science background

Iron combines with oxygen and water to produce rust (iron oxide). If either air or water is absent, iron cannot rust. Stainless steel and brass (drawing pins) are much more resistant to change.

QUESTIONS ⑦ EXTENSIONS ⊖ ASSESSMENT Ⓐ

⑦ Do the iron nails go rusty all over?

⑦ Which nail went rusty quickest?

⑦ Can you make the nail shiny again?

⊖ What happens when you use salt water?

⊖ Find ways to stop nails going rusty when they are wet.

Ⓐ Ask children to tell you about rusty things they have seen.

Metal decay

26

What happens to iron things when they are left out in the rain?

Try different ways to make a nail go rusty. Were your tests fair?

Find out what happens to other metals in the rain.

staples

drawing pins

stainless steel spoon

coins

SPECTRUM SCIENCE

Exploring Life and the Environment
levels 1-3

27 Near the school

Exploring the good and bad effects of human activity on an area

Apparatus

Clipboards and paper

PoS	Level	AT1			AT 2
		i	ii	iii	
2iii	1		a		
	2				
	3				b
	4				
	5				

- Restrict the study to a very small park or small open area near the school. Encourage the children to acknowledge the positive steps taken by people to improve the environment. What jobs do people do every day? Every week? Once a month? If workpeople are in the area, ask them to talk about their job. Local park supervisors may be keen to encourage a positive attitude to public amenities and may visit school if invited.

- Make a class book about the area. Include reports of interviews with people who use the area. Draw a sketch map recording some of the good and bad human influences on the area. List good and bad influences.

Science background

Some of the litter left by people or their animals can be hazardous. Broken glass and ripped drinks cans cause cuts. Dog faeces can be infected with parasitic worms which can cause illness. Accumulations of litter occur where there is shelter from the wind. Hedges and long grass physically stop the litter from blowing away.

QUESTIONS ⑦ EXTENSIONS ⊖ ASSESSMENT Ⓐ

⑦ Why do paths get worn in the grass?

⑦ Are the trees and bushes looked after? How can you tell?

⊖ Use a camera to record what you notice.

⊖ Find out about the history of the area by asking old people and looking at maps.

Ⓐ Write a story about what would happen to the area if people stopped looking after it.

Near the school

27

Visit a grassy area with your teacher.

What have people done to make the area good to visit?

Draw the things you notice.

made benches

planted trees

planted flowers

What have some people done to spoil the area?

SPECTRUM SCIENCE

Exploring Life and the Environment
levels 1-3

28 Growing trees and wild flowers

Growing and planting tree seedlings to help in long term
environmental improvement
Planting native wild flowers to encourage a range of insects
Re-using containers

PoS	Level	AT1 i	ii	iii	AT 2
	1	a			
2iii	2				
	3				b
	4				
	5				

Apparatus

Tree seeds
Wild flower seeds
Soil
Compost
Pots and re-usable containers

- Ask the children about places in the locality or school where trees and wild flowers would improve the environment.

- Collect or buy tree seeds and wild flower seeds from seed merchants (e.g. Suttons, Torquay TQ2 7QJ). You may be able to obtain them from gardens or your local Parks Department.

- Display, sort and name the seeds. Plant three seeds to one cup; if all come up transplant two. There will probably be weed seeds in the soil already. Keep the pots moist. Drainage holes are vital as are trays to catch the drips.

- Give away the plants or sell them at school fairs. The children could research the eventual height and spread of the trees using secondary sources to advise on suitable planting positions.

- Alternatively, plant the plants in an area of ground near the school or in the grounds where they will improve the environment.

Science background

Some seeds need a period of cold before they will germinate. The first seed leaves on most plants are unlike the mature leaves. Once three sets have been produced you can check their identity. Planting wild flowers as plants rather than seeds gives them some chance to compete with the other flora. Pull up competing weeds by hand.

QUESTIONS ⑦ EXTENSIONS ⊖ ASSESSMENT Ⓐ

⑦ How do you think plants spread naturally?

⑦ How can you stop the flowers from being choked by weeds?

⊖ Devise a way of watering the plants in the holidays.

⊖ Draw plans showing how an area near the school could be improved by careful planting.

Ⓐ Draw a picture showing what the area might look like in a few years time.

Growing trees and wild flowers

pine seed

conkers

poppy seeds.

teasel seeds

ash seeds.

acorns

mountain ash berries

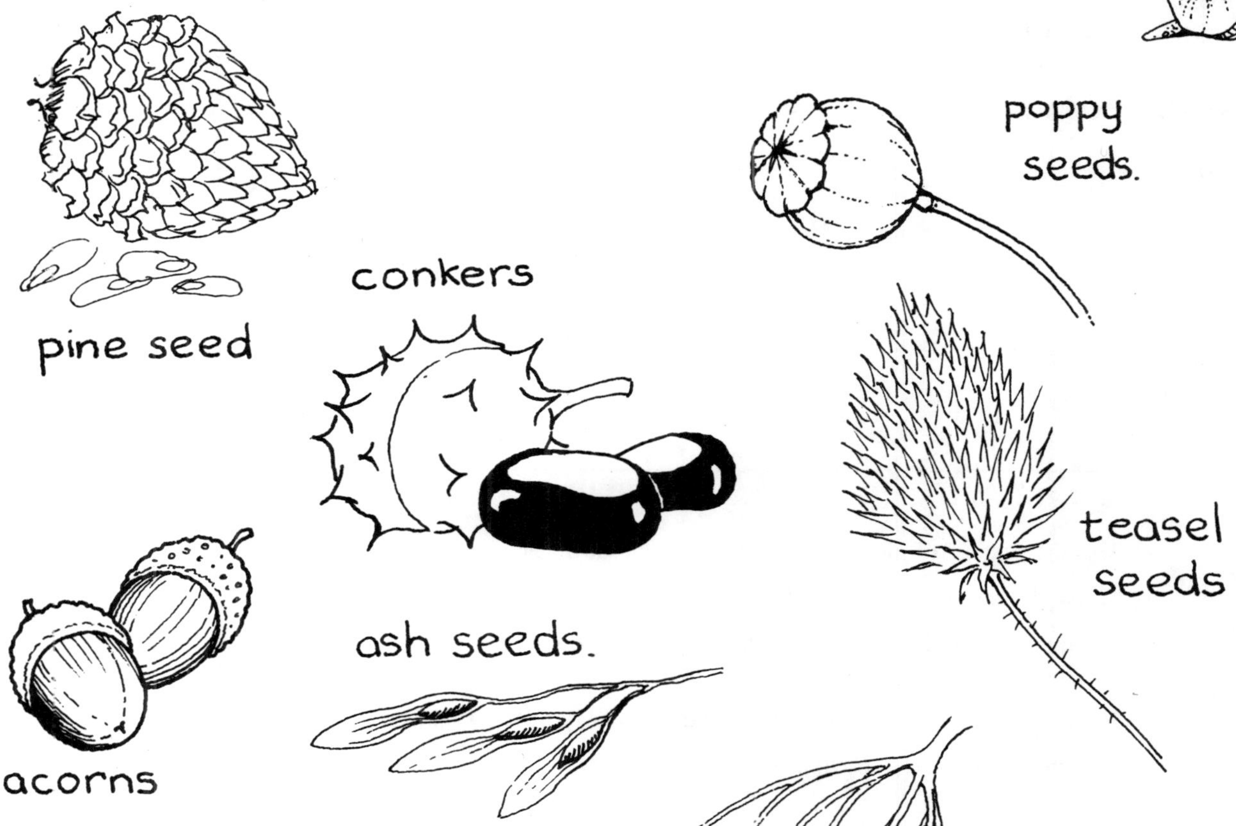

Make a collection of tree seeds or wild flower seeds.

Draw the seeds and their containers.

Grow your seeds in pots.

Where can you put the small plants to improve the area near your school?

SPECTRUM SCIENCE

Exploring Life and the Environment levels 1-3

29 Today's weather

Identifying weather from pictures
Keeping a pictorial record of the weather over a period of time

Apparatus

Drawing materials

PoS	Level	AT1			AT G1
		i	ii	iii	
5c 4v	1		a		
	2				d
	3				
	4				
	5				

- Use the first set of pictures as starting points for discussion.

- Draw children's attention to different features of the weather and what it feels like.

- Arrange the children's weather pictures in chronological order. This is especially effective if the weather is changeable.

- Put a caption below each picture including the day of the week. Link with sequencing in maths.

 - Present in the form of a zig zag book.

Science background

Weather changes are related to the movement of large masses of air. Large high pressure areas bring periods of settled weather with little wind. Low pressure areas produce very varied weather since there are zones of warm wet air and zones of cold air. Homemade ways of predicting weather, such as seaweed, rely on the changing humidity of the air. Barometers measure the pressure of the air.

QUESTIONS ⑦ EXTENSIONS ⊖ ASSESSMENT Ⓐ

⑦ What was the weather like yesterday?

⑦ What do you think the weather will be like tomorrow?

⑦ What was the weather like on Monday? Wednesday?

⊖ Draw pictures of things people like doing in different weather.

Ⓐ Can children tell you about their favourite sort of weather?

Today's weather

29

What is the weather like in these pictures?

Draw a picture of
the weather today.

Draw more
pictures when the
weather changes.

SPECTRUM
SCIENCE

Exploring Life and
the Environment
levels 1-3

30 Windy weather

Exploring the effects of the wind using simple objects

Apparatus

Collection of plastic bottles and other containers
Variety of balls

PoS	Level	AT1			AT G1
		i	ii	iii	
5c	1				
4v	2	a	b		d
	3				
	4				
	5				

- A fairly light wind is best for these activities.
- Too strong a wind may blow the objects too far too fast. Start with plastic containers as suggested and then try balls of different sizes and types.
- Draw pictures of 'things the wind will move' and 'things the wind can't move'.

Science background

Wind is moving air. It pushes against objects which will move if the force is strong enough. Objects which are light for their size are likely to be moved by the wind.

QUESTIONS ⑦ EXTENSIONS ⊖ ASSESSMENT Ⓐ

⑦ What is knocking the bottles over?

⑦ When they fall, do they all fall the same way?

⊖ Put water in the bottles. Do they still blow over?

⊖ Attach a piece of card to a stable bottle. Does it fall over now?

Ⓐ Ask the children to talk about other effects of the wind.

Windy weather

30

Put some plastic containers in a windy place.

Which ones fall over?

Can you find a place where they all stand up?

What other things can the wind move?

SPECTRUM
SCIENCE

*Exploring Life and
the Environment*
levels 1-3

31   Weather chart

Using a simple chart to record changes in the weather

Apparatus

Paper and pencils

PoS	Level	AT1			AT G1
		i	ii	iii	
5c	1				
4v	2		b		d
	3				
	4				
	5				

- Tell children never to look directly at the sun.

- You could make a larger wall version of the chart which two or three children could complete each day. The children could draw the pictures for the left hand column.

- Talk about the best time of day to tick the chart.

Science background

White cloud types include 'cumulus', the fluffy fair weather cloud and 'cirrus', the high altitude wispy cloud. 'Nimbostratus' is the dark grey blanket cloud which brings steady rain.

QUESTIONS ⑦ EXTENSIONS ⊖ ASSESSMENT Ⓐ

⑦ What sort of clouds seem to give rain?

⑦ What has been the most common weather this week?

⑦ Are the clouds low or very high up?

⑦ How long was it sunny today?

⊖ Paint cloudscapes.

⊖ Keep a weather diary.

Ⓐ Can the children tell you about the weather?

Weather chart

31

Tick the right box or boxes.

Can you see?	Monday	Tuesday	Wednesday	Thursday	Friday
white cloud					
dark cloud					
rain					
sun					
fog					
Snow					

SPECTRUM SCIENCE

Exploring Life and the Environment levels 1-3

32 Sorting rocks

Sorting rocks according to observable features

Apparatus

Sufficient variety of rocks for children working in groups (or other natural material)
Lenses
Droppers
Large sheets of paper

Plasticine, plaster of Paris – extension activities

PoS	Level	AT1			AT 3
		i	ii	iii	
	1				
3iv	2		b		a
	3				
	4				
	5				

- Give each child in the group one rock to talk about.

- The children should work in groups of four to six so that they have sufficient rocks to sort.

- Try to obtain some contrasting rock specimens. If rock specimens are not available, you could use wood, shells or feathers. The more able children should take the last turn when sorting into groups. Play 'guess the rock' in which one child thinks of a rock and responds yes or no to questions from the others. Have hand lenses available to look at details. Identification books may be helpful but naming rocks is very difficult.

- Draw the two groups of rocks. Display with a caption.

Science background

Rocks formed from volcanic activity are referred to as igneous rocks. They sometimes exhibit large interlocking crystals (e.g. granite). Sedimentary rocks are formed when sediment is deposited in water. Common rocks include chalk and slate. At this stage it is unimportant what rock types you have as long as there is a variety.

QUESTIONS ⑦ EXTENSIONS ⊖ ASSESSMENT Ⓐ

⑦ What happens when you put a drop of water on each specimen?

⑦ Does the rock make a mark on the playground?

⊖ Look at building materials. Concrete and bricks are manufactured rocks. Which materials are used in an unaltered state?

⊖ Look for fossils. Make artificial fossils using Plasticine and plaster of Paris.

Ⓐ Can the children pick an odd one out from a set of four rocks. Three of the rocks should share an obvious attribute.

Sorting rocks

32

Look closely at
a rock.

Take turns to
describe your
rock.

Is it heavy?
Is it hard?
Are there any shiny pieces?
Is it rough?
Are there any sharp edges?
What colour is it?

Sort all your
rocks into
two groups.

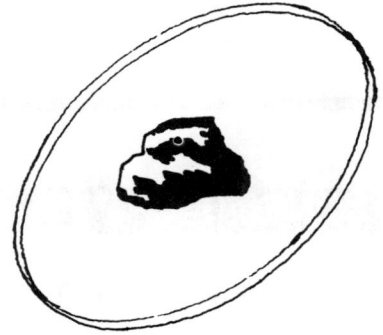

Take turns to group them in other ways.

SPECTRUM
SCIENCE

*Exploring Life and
the Environment*
levels 1-3

33   Rock trees

Sorting rocks using branching sets

Apparatus

Rocks (or other natural material)
Large sheet of paper
Lenses

Branch and Sort (software) – extension activities

PoS	Level	AT1			AT 3
		i	ii	iii	
	1				
3iv	2		b		a
	3				
	4				
	5				

- This sheet develops activity 32.
  Any other natural material or a variety of materials could be used. The children could take turns to divide the sets. Use the 'tree' to help describe the rocks. For instance in the illustrated example the rock in the bottom left is hard and shiny.

- The most important part of the activity is posing good questions with yes or no answers.

 • Draw out the 'trees' on better quality paper with observational drawings at the end of each branch.

Science background

Classification keys are introduced in Key Stage 2 but this is useful preparatory work.

QUESTIONS ⑦ EXTENSIONS ⊖ ASSESSMENT Ⓐ

⑦   Which rock is soft and shiny? (Change the question to suit the 'tree'.)

⑦   Make a set of three rocks. Which is the odd one out?

⊖   Use a computer program such as *Branch and Sort* once the children are familiar with the activity on paper.

Ⓐ   Can the children make a branching tree with three objects and explain how they did it?

Rock trees

33

Draw a circle round four or five rocks on a big sheet of paper.

Ask a question which will split them into two groups.

Is it shiny?

Yes   No

Ask a question which will split one group into two.

Is it hard?

Yes   No

Now do the same on the other branch of the sorting tree.

SPECTRUM SCIENCE

Exploring Life and the Environment
levels 1-3

34 Hard rock

Designing and carrying out a variety of hardness tests on rock

Apparatus

Lenses
Rocks
Steel screws
Iron nails
Coins
Metre rule

PoS	Level	AT1 i	ii	iii	AT 3
3iv	1				
	2				a
	3	a	b	c	
	4				
	5				

- At first pupils may be confused about the term hardness. Ask them to explain their ideas to you before they do the experiments.

- A similar investigation could be done using wood e.g. balsa, pine, oak or other hardwood.

- Only use rock samples which have no great beauty. Ensure a good range from very soft to hard.

- Invent a name for rocks you are not sure of. Make a simple table of results.

Rock	Could it be scratched by			
	Fingernail	Coin	Nail	Steel screw
Sandstone	no	no	yes	yes

Science background

The hardness of rocks is measured on Moh's scale ranging from talc which has a hardness of 1, to diamond with a hardness of 10. The best test of hardness is to systematically try to scratch the rock with progressively harder implements. Start with a fingernail, then a coin, a nail and finally a steel screw. Use a lens to check that the rock is really scratched, not simply marked.

QUESTIONS ⑦ EXTENSIONS ⊖ ASSESSMENT Ⓐ

⑦ Is the rock the same hardness all over?

⑦ Are the heavy rocks harder than the lighter ones?

⊖ Look at how stone used in building has been eroded.

Ⓐ Can the children explain how they would investigate the hardness of different floor coverings?

Hard rock

34

Feel four different pieces of rock.

Which is hardest?

Put all four in order of hardness.

Design a hardness test.

Here is one idea.

How will you make your test fair?

Scratch each rock with a nail.
How deep is the scratch?

SPECTRUM
SCIENCE

*Exploring Life and
the Environment*
levels 1-3

35   Soil

Investigating samples of soil from different places

Apparatus

Trowel
Plates
Lenses
Microscope
Small plastic bags (e.g. sandwich bags) or small plastic boxes

Scales – extension activity

PoS	Level	AT1 i	AT1 ii	AT1 iii	AT 3
	1				
3iv	2		b		a
	3				
	4				
	5				

- Cover the table with a cloth or large sheets of paper.

- Ask the children to bring soil samples from their own gardens if they have them. If your locality is suitable, take the children for a walk to collect soil samples from contrasting environments. Use a spade to remove turf if you want soil from a grassy field. (Take care not to gather dog mess with the soil!)

- Divide a sheet of paper in two by folding. Make notes about two soils using the questions opposite as a structure. Use the notes as the basis of a more extended piece of writing.

Science background

Soil is simply ground up rock mixed with plant remains. It varies from place to place, influenced largely by the underlying rock. Chalk soils, for instance, are thin and stony. Clay soils are heavy and form balls very easily. Soil from below established park trees and hedges may be very dusty due to the absence of humus. Woodland soils are rich in humus as a result of the build-up of leaf mould.

QUESTIONS ⑦ EXTENSIONS ⊖ ASSESSMENT Ⓐ

⑦ Which soil sticks together when you squeeze it?

⑦ What does the soil look like under the microscope?

⊖ Weigh 100g of each soil. Allow to dry. Which contains most water?

⊖ Put soil samples in plant pots. Water them. Does anything grow?

Ⓐ Can the children tell you about two places with different soil types?

Soil

35

Collect samples of soil from different places,
such as
around school
under a hedge
a garden
waste ground
a wood

Display your soil on plates with a label saying
where it came from.

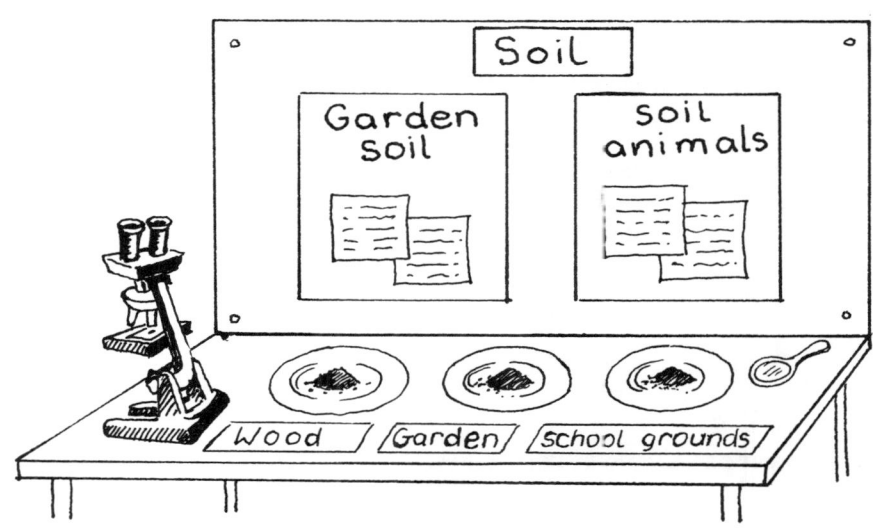

What differences can you
smell? feel? see?

What animal or plant remains can you find?
Use a lens or microscope to help you.

SPECTRUM
SCIENCE

*Exploring Life and
the Environment*
levels 1-3

36   Soil grains

Investigating the different grain sizes of a variety of soils

Apparatus

Soil samples (include a variety)
Spoons
Jam jars and lids

Sieves – extension activities

PoS	Level	AT1			AT 3
		i	ii	iii	
3iv	1				
	2		b		a
	3			d	
	4				
	5				

- This activity could follow 35. Use aprons if available.

- Include potting compost or leaf mould in your tests. These contain large amounts of plant remains (humus) which float on the surface.

- Encourage the children to put down the jars immediately after shaking as this helps the layers to form.

- Record the whole investigation in cartoon form using a piece of A3 paper folded in 6 or 8 to sequence the different stages of the work.

Science background

Most soils contain a mixture of clay particles, some sand, stones and plant material (humus). The particles of sand and the stones sink rapidly but the finer clay particles settle very slowly. Soil from the bottom of a hole contains more stones and less humus than topsoil.

QUESTIONS ⑦ EXTENSIONS ⊖ ASSESSMENT Ⓐ

⑦ Which bits sank first?

⑦ Why do you think the bigger pieces fall first?

⑦ How long do you think it will take for the water to clear?

⊖ Sieve the soil using different grades of mesh.

⊖ Dig a deep hole. Compare the soil from the bottom with the topsoil.

Ⓐ Can the children tell you about what soil is made from?

Soil grains

36

Put two big spoons of one kind of soil in a jar.

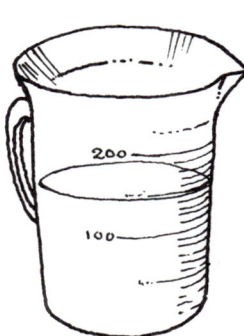

Label it.

Half-fill it with water.

Put the lid on tight and shake the jar.

Let the soil settle.

Which layer has the biggest pieces?

Which layer has the smallest pieces?

Do the same for other soils.

Can you say why the layers form as they do?

SPECTRUM SCIENCE

Exploring Life and the Environment levels 1-3

37 Home-made soil

Making different types of soil from broken or weathered rock and plant remains
Investigating their qualities as a growing medium

Apparatus

Microscope
Plant pots and saucers
Commercial composts, peat, sand, dry clay, seeds

Hammer, soft rocks, safety glasses – extension activity

PoS	Level	AT1			AT 3
		i	ii	iii	
	1				
3iv	2				
	3		c	d	c
	4				
	5				

• Break up the dry clay in plastic bags outside to minimise dust. Do not let children breathe it. If necessary show children how to view small amounts under the microscope without dirtying the objective lens.

• Provide enough of each soil so that children can measure and mix different soils as suggested on the pupil's page. Ask them to measure accurately using the standard measures available in the classroom. Compare the mixtures with commercial composts.

• Drawings of what they observe down the microscope could be put in a book with results of other investigations. The growth of seeds in each sort of soil could be graphed.

Science background

John Innes compost is based on soil. Peat-based composts combine sharp grit and peat. Peat is the result of partial decay of bog plants. It is being used up and the wildlife of bogs is dwindling. The only plants that can live on pure rock are algae and lichens. However, many appear to as they grow in cracks in walls or paths.

QUESTIONS ⑦ EXTENSIONS ⊖ ASSESSMENT Ⓐ

⑦ Which home-made soils form into balls when you squeeze them?

⑦ Does using gritty sand or fine silver sand make any difference?

⊖ Visit a garden centre to see how they mix and use composts.

⊖ Compare how quickly the children's mixtures drain.

⊖ Pound a piece of soft rock with a hammer. Wear safety glasses and enclose the rock. See if any seeds grow in the bits produced.

Ⓐ Can children explain how soil is formed and how their soils differ?

Home-made soil

37

Look closely at a
few bits of sand,
clay and peat.

Sand is rock which has been
broken down into grains.

Clay is rock which has been
broken down to very fine
dust.

Peat is made from plant
remains.

Make different kinds of soil by mixing different
amounts of sand, dry clay and peat.

1 peat
1 sand

1 clay
1 sand

2 sand
1 peat

Design a test to see which mixture grows seeds
best. Was your test fair?

SPECTRUM
SCIENCE

Exploring Life and
the Environment
levels 1-3

38 Hot and cold

Extending experiences of hot and cold toward the idea of a scale
of temperature

Apparatus

A cold day!
Pictures of hot and cold situations and objects
Advertisements for food as a source of warmth

PoS	Level	AT1			AT 4
		i	ii	iii	
4ii	1		a		
	2				b
	3				
	4				
	5				

- Wintry weather could stimulate this. Cold and warm things might be useful to refer to but it would be best to follow up real experiences – for instance warming up after a cold playtime.

- Warn children of the dangers of very hot things and of getting too cold or hot themselves.

- Drawing or cutting out pictures can prompt comparison of how cold or hot things are. Children may see coldness and hotness as distinct things and use terms in quite unscientific ways. Help them begin to use words more accurately.

- The sequencing should help them build their understanding of relative hotness. Display their pictures as a strip to emphasise this.

Science background

People need to maintain a constant body temperature. In cold weather we lose heat quickly as heat travels from hotter to colder things. Insulation can reduce the rate at which this happens.

QUESTIONS ⑦ EXTENSIONS ⊖ ASSESSMENT Ⓐ

⑦ How do you keep warm in cold weather?

⑦ What's the hottest thing you know/the coldest?

⑦ Which things are hotter than you/colder than you?

⊖ Try to space their pictures to indicate relative hotness. Colour code them.

⊖ Add pictures or words to say what happens at points on the scale.

Ⓐ Do children realise that cold and hot are part of a continuum or do they believe that 'the cold' is a separate thing from heat?

Hot and cold

38

How can you tell this is a cold day?

Make pictures of some hot things and some cold things.

Put your pictures in order from coldest to hottest, like these:

SPECTRUM SCIENCE

Exploring Life and the Environment
levels 1-3

39 How warm?

Comparing hot and cold
Estimating and measuring temperatures

Apparatus

4 bowls
Ice cubes (optional)
Cold and hand-hot water
Towel
Jug
Thermometers (Do not use mercury filled ones. Strip thermometers will
do if they cover the right range of temperature. Wall-hanging
thermometers with spirit in – usually red – are convenient and sturdy).

PoS	Level	AT1			AT 4
		i	ii	iii	
	1				
4ii	2				b
	3	a	b		
	4				
	5				

 • Warn pupils not to feel very hot things.

• You could start with a demonstration of the activity on the pupil's sheet, and then give a small group icy water in one bowl and hand-hot in another. If children are not familiar with thermometers you will need to show them how to use them correctly.

• Ask the group to compare and talk about their judgements of how 'warm' each feels. Get them to decide on the best words to describe each.

• Encourage the idea of a scale of hotness rather than simply hot or cold. Mixing water to get intermediate temperatures will help here.

• Grading and comparing close temperatures leads to the need for a thermometer. Ensure children leave the thermometers in each bowl long enough.

 • Accurate records are less important than careful observation at first. Children's observations can be structured using simple tables.

Science background

Temperature is a measure of how hot something is. We can estimate relative hotness and detect changes by feeling. Accurate measurement of temperature requires a thermometer.

QUESTIONS ⑦ EXTENSIONS ⊖ ASSESSMENT Ⓐ

⑦ How warm does it feel?

⑦ Is this much hotter than that?

⑦ Can you mix water that is halfway between the hot and cold?

⊖ Mix different proportions of icy and hot water. Help children read the temperatures of the mixtures.

⊖ Measure hot, cold and lukewarm water at intervals to see how they change.

Ⓐ Do children know what a thermometer does? Can they use it carefully?

How warm?

39

Feel the cold water.

Feel the warm water.

Mix a little of each in an empty bowl.

How warm does the mixture feel?

Now use a thermometer to measure the temperature in each bowl.

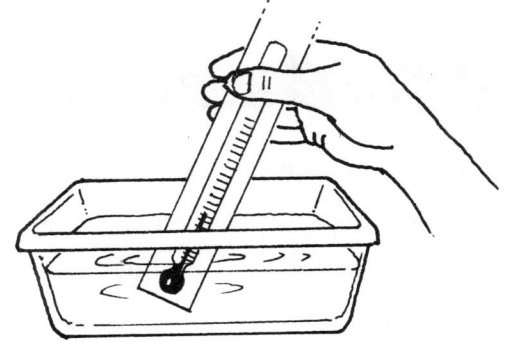

SPECTRUM SCIENCE

Exploring Life and the Environment
levels 1-3

40 Thermometers

Measuring temperature

Apparatus

Thermometers (see notes)
Containers for liquids

PoS	Level	AT1 i	AT1 ii	AT1 iii	AT 4
4ii	1				
	2	a			b
	3		b		
	4				
	5				

 • Take care that the tap water is not above hand-hot. It will damage both the children and the recommended thermometer if it is hotter than 50°C.

 • The best thermometers for use in the classroom are alcohol-filled with a robust clearly calibrated case. They should measure the range between -10°C and 50°C at least. Never use mercury thermometers.

• The correct unit of temperature is degrees Celsius, Centigrade can be any 100-point scale.

• Show the children how to read the temperature by looking straight on at the thermometer. If you look at an angle the reading is incorrect.

• The ice and salt mix will give temperatures lower than 0°C. The explanation for this is too complex to give here. Most children will just be astonished to record temperatures lower than 0°C.

 • Draw a sketch map of the classroom. Record the temperature in different places on the map. Graph the temperature changes during the day.

Science background

Celsius is a temperature scale with two fixed points. One is the boiling point of water which is 100°C; the other is the melting point of ice which is 0°C. All other temperatures on the scale are fixed in relation to these.

QUESTIONS ⑦ EXTENSIONS ⊖ ASSESSMENT Ⓐ

⑦ Which do you think is the warmest place in the school?

⑦ Do you need to leave the thermometer in a place for a little time before taking the reading?

⑦ Which temperatures did you find difficult to estimate?

⊖ Measure and graph the temperature throughout a whole day.

⊖ Use computer sensors which are available from several suppliers to record the changes in temperature; during the day; as water is heated; as warm water cools in insulation experiments; as ice melts.

Ⓐ Use the initial activity on the pupil's sheet to diagnose those children who need direct instruction on reading from scales.

Thermometers

40

What is the temperature shown on these six thermometers?

| 1 | 2 | 3 | 4 | 5 | 6 |

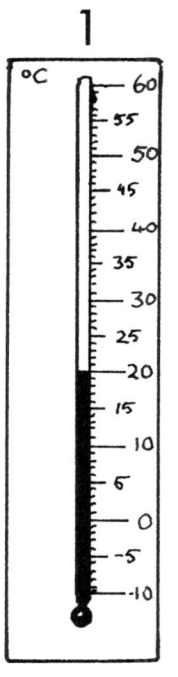 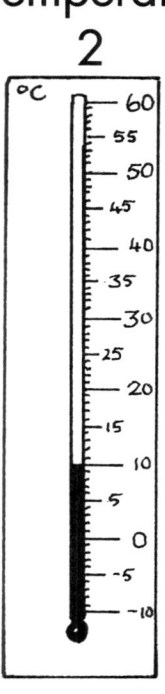 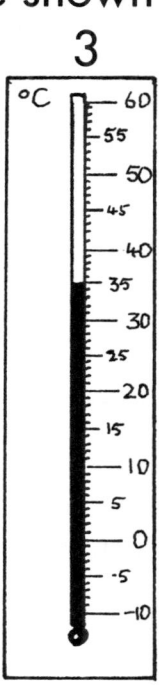 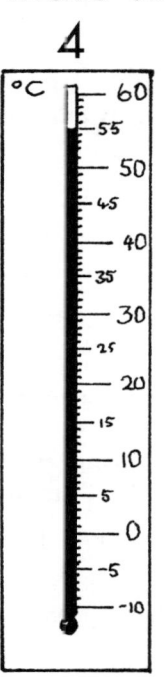 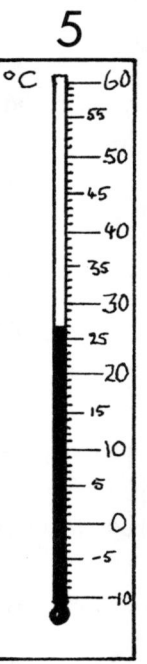 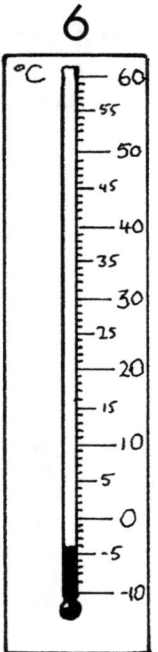

__20°C__ _____ _____ _____ _____ _____

Use a thermometer to measure the temperature in different places.

Estimate the temperature first.

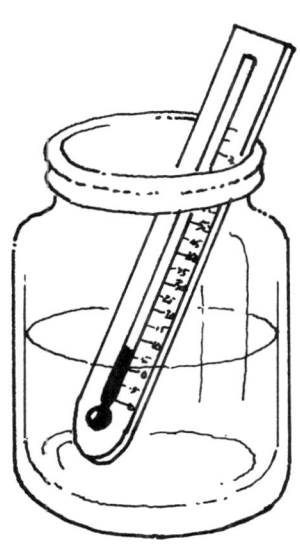

Place	Temperature	
	estimate	actual
in the classroom		
near the door		
above the radiator		

Measure the temperature of liquids like:

cold tap water _____

hot tap water _____

ice and water _____

ice and salty water _____

SPECTRUM SCIENCE

Exploring Life and the Environment levels 1-3

41   Fuels

Fuels are used to produce movement and heat

Apparatus

A range of food packages showing energy information

PoS	Level	AT1 i	AT1 ii	AT1 iii	AT 4
4ii	1				
	2		b		
	3				b
	4				
	5				

- Use a range of packets with energy information. Tell the children that eating too much high energy foods, e.g. crisps, could lead to them storing the energy they don't use as fat.

- Talk about the whole range of fuels that the children have heard of. Make a wall display of energy sources.

- Draw pictures showing what happens to the fuels when they are used. e.g.

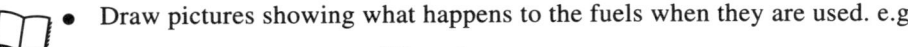

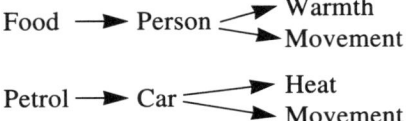

Science background

Fuel provides the energy for movement and keeping warm. Fuel can either be burnt as in the case of gas, petrol, coal and wood, or it can be used by living things in respiration. Respiration is a slower release of the energy in a fuel. Both respiration and burning result in the same amount of heat energy being released. If a peanut is burnt and used to heat a tube of water, the same amount of heat is released as in our bodies when it is eaten. High energy foods include oils, fats and sugars. Fuel is a form of stored energy. Even though we say it is 'used', it is actually converted into other forms of energy, usually heat or movement.

QUESTIONS ⑦ EXTENSIONS ⊖ ASSESSMENT Ⓐ

⑦ Which food fills you up and gives you lots of energy?

⑦ Which foods would make you fat if you ate too much of them?

⑦ Which fuels do you use at home? How do you heat your house?

⊖ Graph the sorts of fuels used to heat pupils' homes. Graph the number of people who use food energy to get to school (walking) and those who use petrol energy.

⊖ Burn small pieces of food such as peanuts, sugar and raisins on spoons made from pieces of foil held over a nightlight flame with a wooden peg.

Ⓐ Ask the children to tell you about the fuels they have used during the day. What keeps them warm and how have they moved around?

Fuels

41

Draw a line from the object to the fuel it uses.

Complete these sentences.

1 The fuel for cars is _____.

2 Wood is the fuel for _____.

3 A camping stove uses _____.

4 A steam engine uses _____ for fuel.

5 The fuel for people is _____.

Look at packets of food.

List the amount of energy you get from eating them.

Which food has most food energy?

Food Energy		
Food	Amount	Energy (k. Joules)
Cornflakes	100 g	1650
Baked beans	100 g	306

SPECTRUM
SCIENCE

*Exploring Life and
the Environment*
levels 1-3

42 The seasons

Talking about the differences between seasons using pictures and postcards as prompts

PoS
5c 4v

Level	AT1 i	AT1 ii	AT1 iii	AT G3
1		a		
2				a
3				
4				
5				

Apparatus

Photographs and postcards brought in by the children
Posters

- The larger the group the larger the pictures will need to be.
- Many resorts offer postcards which show the same scene in both summer and winter.
- This activity will introduce talk about the ideas of seasonal change but, as with anything of this kind, the work about seasons should be spread out during the year.
- Recording could be in the form of a display of a selection of pictures with captions done by the teacher scribing the children's own ideas.

Science background

The Earth is tilted on its axis. As it rotates around the Sun, either the northern or southern hemisphere is tilted away from the Sun. When the north is tilted away it has winter and when it is tilted towards the Sun it enjoys summer. Similarly, when the south is tilted away it has its winter and when it is tilted towards the Sun it enjoys summer.

QUESTIONS ? EXTENSIONS → ASSESSMENT Ⓐ

? What sorts of things do you enjoy doing in the summer?

? What is the time of year when there are most flowers?

? At what time of year is it dark when you leave school?

→ Ask the children for summer words and winter words. Write these on strips of paper. Ask the children to put them with the appropriate pictures.

→ Make seasonal displays on a nature table.

Ⓐ Can the children tell you about some of the changes from winter to summer?

The seasons

42

Display photographs and pictures of summer.

Tell the class what you do in summer.

Look at photographs and pictures of winter.

Talk about the differences between them.

84

SPECTRUM SCIENCE

Exploring Life and the Environment
levels 1-3

43   Signs of spring

Observing and recording signs of seasonal change

Apparatus

Tape recorder (useful)
Secateurs
Spade
Tray

Turf, tree twigs – extension activities

PoS	Level	AT1 i	AT1 ii	AT1 iii	AT G3
5c 4v	1		a		
	2				a
	3				
	4				
	5				

- This activity is related to seasonal change and, suitably amended, could be done at different times of the year as part of a year-long study of the seasons or change. The suggestions opposite focus on looking for change on three physical levels. Change at ground level may include growth of grass, daisies and dandelions. Pavements and tarmac may be dry, wormcasts may be visible along with evidence of other tiny animals. The sky may be bright and the sun may be higher. Warn the children not to look directly at the Sun. Trees may be home to birds and the new leaves and flowers may be evident.

- Use a tape recorder to record what children notice and use this to help make notes back in the classroom.

Science background

The Earth is tilted on its axis. When the northern hemisphere is tilted towards the Sun it enjoys summer. In winter the northern hemisphere is tilted away from the Sun. In winter, the Sun is low and visible for a short time. It gives little heat and light. Plants need light and heat to grow. Many animals need food from plants and heat to be active. So in winter there is very little evidence of biological activity. Spring is the time of most obvious change.

QUESTIONS ⑦ EXTENSIONS ⊖ ASSESSMENT Ⓐ

⑦ How has weather changed during the last few weeks?

⑦ What time does it get dark?

⑦ What kind of outdoor clothes are you wearing now?

⑦ Are these things different from last term?

⊖ Cut a square of turf. Bring it indoors to enjoy an accelerated spring. The grass and other plants will grow more rapidly indoors.

⊖ Teacher could use secateurs to cut a few twigs from trees. Put in water and bring indoors (see activity 28).

Ⓐ Ask what sort of weather you expect in summer, autumn, winter and spring. When is it warm? When is it cold?

Signs of spring

43

What signs of spring can you see?

Go out to a park with your teacher or go to the school field if you have one.

Look at the ground.
Look at the sky.
Look on the trees.

List the signs of spring which you notice.

SPECTRUM SCIENCE

Exploring Life and the Environment
levels 1-3

44   The moving Sun

Talking about the apparent movement of the Sun relative to school

Apparatus

None

PoS	Level	AT1			AT 4
		i	ii	iii	
	1				d
4v	2		b		
	3				
	4				
	5				

- Remind the children not to look directly at the Sun.

- The activity provides a starting point for conversation about the apparent daily motion of the Sun across the sky. Talk about what you mean by a room being sunny. What do you mean by shade and what do the children understand by this term?

- When the children have found a place outside which they think will remain in shade all day, they can chalk their names there if it is appropriate. They can go back to check from time to time.

- If the school is a relatively simple shape the children could record their results on a previously drawn sketch plan of the school.

Science background

The Earth rotates in an easterly direction so the Sun appears to rise in the east and set in the west. The time of year affects the angle of the Sun's rays and this will also affect which rooms are sunny and which spots get the Sun at some time during the day. In the northern hemisphere the Sun shines from the south and in the southern hemisphere the Sun shines from the north.

QUESTIONS ② EXTENSIONS ⊖ ASSESSMENT Ⓐ

② Where is the Sun in the sky? Point in its general direction without looking at it directly.

② Can you stand in a place so that all of you is in shade?

② Which rooms in school are hottest? Are these the ones which catch the Sun?

⊖ Read the children the Greek myth of Apollo and the Sun chariot.

⊖ Where do seedlings grow best? Try them in shady rooms and compare them with those grown in the sunny rooms.

Ⓐ Can the children tell you about or show you the way the Sun moves across the sky?

The moving Sun

44

Which rooms in the school are sunny in the morning?

Which rooms are sunny at lunch time?

Which rooms are sunny at home time?

Find a place outside where the Sun never shines.

45 Sunrise and sunset

Recording the time when lights come on and the Sun sets
Looking to see when the sky gets dark enough to see the first star

Apparatus

The lighting up times for your area (usually found with the weather forecast in the newspaper)

PoS	Level	AT1			AT 4
		i	ii	iii	
	1				
4v	2				
	3		b		c
	4				
	5				

- Children who cannot tell the time easily using an analogue clock will probably find this activity easier if a digital clock is used. Try to choose a period when the skies are relatively clear. The best time of year is autumn or spring when the time of sunrise and sunset is changing rapidly. Don't do this at midsummer or near Christmas as you will see relatively little change.

- Children can record their findings on the sheet and you could make a chart showing changes over several weeks.

Science background

The time of sunset gets earlier as the Earth's tilt moves the northern hemisphere away from the Sun. The period of most rapid change is spring or autumn. During these periods the equinoxes occur. These are the days on which the length of day and night are equal. The solstice occurs at midsummer and midwinter and marks the extreme length of day and night.

QUESTIONS ⑦ EXTENSIONS ⊖ ASSESSMENT Ⓐ

⑦ Do you need the light on in the morning all the year round?

⑦ Are there any times in the year when you go to bed in the light?

⑦ How long can you play at this time of year? Is it the same all year?

⊖ Read 'Moomintroll' stories about the land of the midnight sun. Would the children like it if the Sun never set?

⊖ Talk about how the streetlights know when to switch off and on if the time of sunrise and sunset are always changing. You could get the children to write to the local highways department asking them how they do it.

Ⓐ Ask the children to draw two pictures: one showing 'Me getting up in winter' and the other showing 'Me getting up in the summer'. Use these as starting points for assessment of the children's understanding.

What time does the Sun set and it gets dark?

 pm

What time do the street lights come on today?

 pm

When can you see the first star?

☐ pm

Write down the times these things happen next week.

Are the days getting longer or shorter?

SPECTRUM SCIENCE

Exploring Life and the Environment levels 1-3

Recording what the children know about the Earth, Sun and Moon

Apparatus

A globe of the Earth

PoS	Level	AT1			AT 4
		i	ii	iii	
	1				
4v	2		b		e
	3				
	4				
	5				

- The children will probably already know a good deal about the Earth, Sun and Moon from watching television and films. One possible starting point is to show the children the globe of the Earth. Talk about what they know about the Earth. This is a topic which needs a range of secondary sources. These should be ordered well in advance if possible.

- You could make a chart with headings for Sun Facts, Moon Facts and Earth Facts. This could be done on a wall or you could write it as a word processor file for the computer. Begin a simple database showing facts about the three bodies.

Science background

The Earth is considerably bigger than the moon but it is tiny compared with the Sun. The Sun is a ball of hot gas which provides all our heat and light. A spacecraft would be destroyed long before it could approach the Sun closely. The Earth is the only planet to have water on its surface and it is the only one in our solar system known to support life.

QUESTIONS ⑦ EXTENSIONS ⊖ ASSESSMENT Ⓐ

⑦ Do you know what the green parts on this globe are? What are the blue areas?

⑦ What do you think you would need to take with you if you went to the Moon?

⑦ Do you think it would be possible to travel to the Sun?

⊖ Read *The Iron Man* by Ted Hughes. Talk about where the creature could have come from. Could it really have landed on the Sun?

⊖ Write a story about a journey to the Moon or another planet.

Ⓐ Ask the children to do simple spider diagrams with words and ideas they associate with Sun, Moon and Earth.

Earth, Sun and Moon

Draw space rockets to the right place.

Earth

Moon

Sun

People live on it.

It is a hot ball of gas.

There is lots of water on it.

It looks silvery from the Earth.

Animals and plants live on it.

It looks yellow from Earth.

It gives out heat and light.

It is smaller than the Earth.

It is huge compared with the Earth.

SPECTRUM SCIENCE

Exploring Life and the Environment levels 1-3

47

Night and day

Investigating how night and day happen

Apparatus

Small globe (mounted so that it can turn easily)
Strong torch

PoS	Level	AT1			AT 4
		i	ii	iii	
4v	1				
	2		b		
	3	a			
	4				e
	5				

- This activity contains some very complex ideas and children will need to know about the Earth and the Sun as separate bodies before you begin this work. Ask the children about where they live. Ask them to include the country and then the world.

- The children could draw three pictures showing i) people getting up, ii) people working, iii) people sleeping. The children can place these on the globe in appropriate locations according to where the torch is illuminating. Make sure that the labels will not harm the surface of the globe when they are removed.

Science background

The Earth spins round once every 24 hours. Places on the equator are moving at over 1500 km per hour. We cannot feel this motion because we are moving at the same speed and the Earth is neither speeding up nor slowing down. We can only detect this motion by the apparent movement of the Sun across the sky.

QUESTIONS ⑦ EXTENSIONS ⊖ ASSESSMENT Ⓐ

⑦ What gives the Earth heat and light?

⑦ What shape is the Earth?

⑦ Can you feel the Earth spinning round?

⊖ Why can we only see stars at night? Can the children design an investigation to answer this? Take care not to shine very bright lights into eyes.

⊖ What time is it now in other parts of the world?

Ⓐ Show the children Australia and Britain on the globe. Ask them why it would be thoughtless to phone someone in Australia just after our lunchtime.

Shine a torch
at a globe.

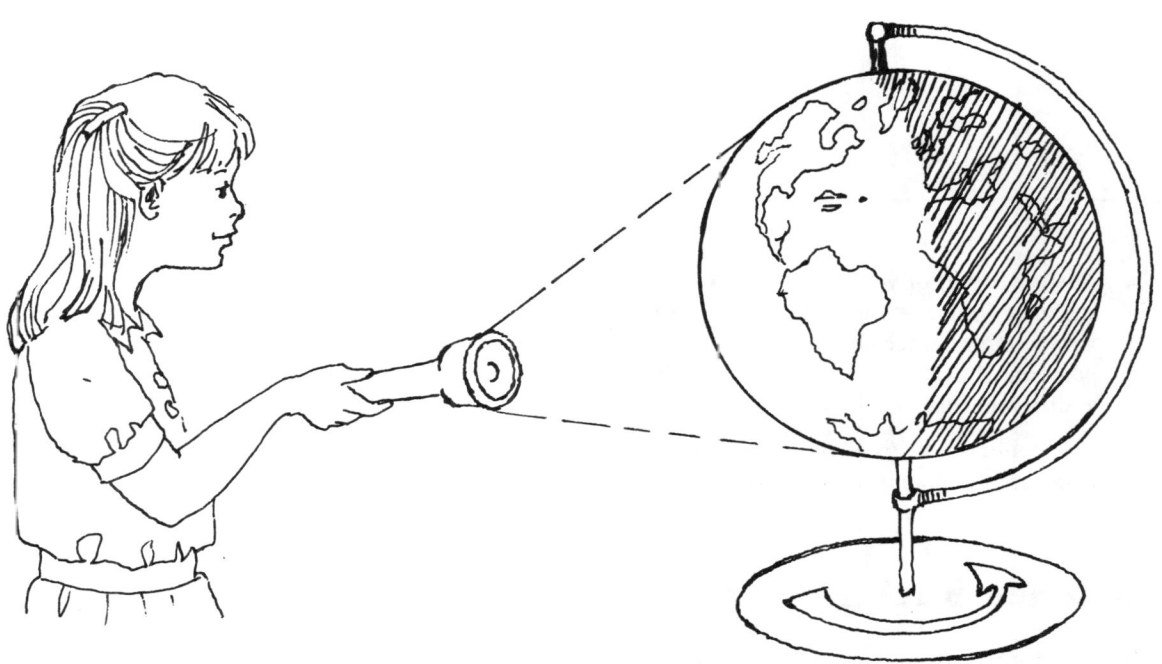

Turn the globe the way the arrow shows.

Stop when your country is lit by the torch.

What do you notice about countries on the other side of the globe?

Turn the globe slowly.

Where is it evening?

Where is it night?

SPECTRUM SCIENCE

Exploring Life and the Environment
levels 1-3

48 Shadow clock

Measuring time with a shadow clock

Apparatus

A skittle, stick or weighted plastic bottle
Large sheet of paper
Compass (see questions)

PoS	Level	AT1			AT 4
		i	ii	iii	
	1				
4v	2				
	3	a	b		
	4				e
	5				

- The best times of year for this work are autumn and spring when the changes in the length of shadows from one week to the next are most pronounced. The concepts underlying this activity are very complex since they involve relating ideas to do with motion, time, light, shadow and relative position. However, most children will be able to appreciate the impressive changes in the shadow at different times of the day.

- You could cut strips of coloured paper the length of each shadow and display these as a graph. Compare the graphs obtained when you repeat the activity a week later. The children could write a brief commentary.

Science background

The Earth rotates on its axis in an easterly direction. This causes the Sun to appear to move across the sky. Light travels in straight lines from the Sun and shadows are made when the light is blocked by an object. Shadows get shorter as the Sun gets higher in the sky and they lengthen as the Sun gets lower in the sky. The Sun is at its highest at midsummer and the shadows it makes are short. In midwinter the Sun is very low in the sky: consequently the shadows are very long.

QUESTIONS ⑦ EXTENSIONS ⊖ ASSESSMENT Ⓐ

⑦ Do you think you could use this idea to tell the time?

⑦ What would be the problems with using a device like this to tell the time?

⑦ From which compass direction is the Sun shining?

⊖ Set up a mirror on the windowsill so that it reflects the Sun onto a wall. Every hour place a sticker on the place where the reflection has reached. Write the time on the sticker. Repeat this activity about a week later and note any differences.

Ⓐ Show the children some shadow clock drawings. Ask them to point to the ones that they think were drawn around shadows in the morning and those on the same sheet which were done at midday. Ask them to try to explain the reasons behind their answer.

Shadow clock

Wait for a sunny day.

Stand a skittle or a stick on a piece of paper.

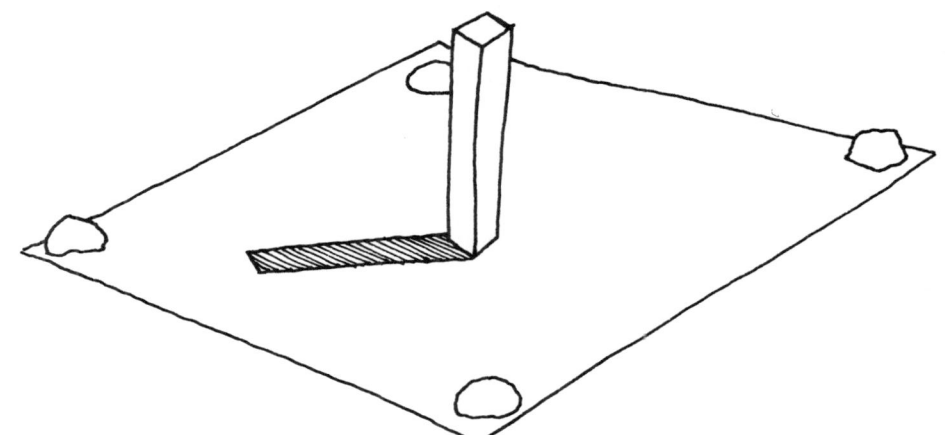

Draw round the shadow every hour.

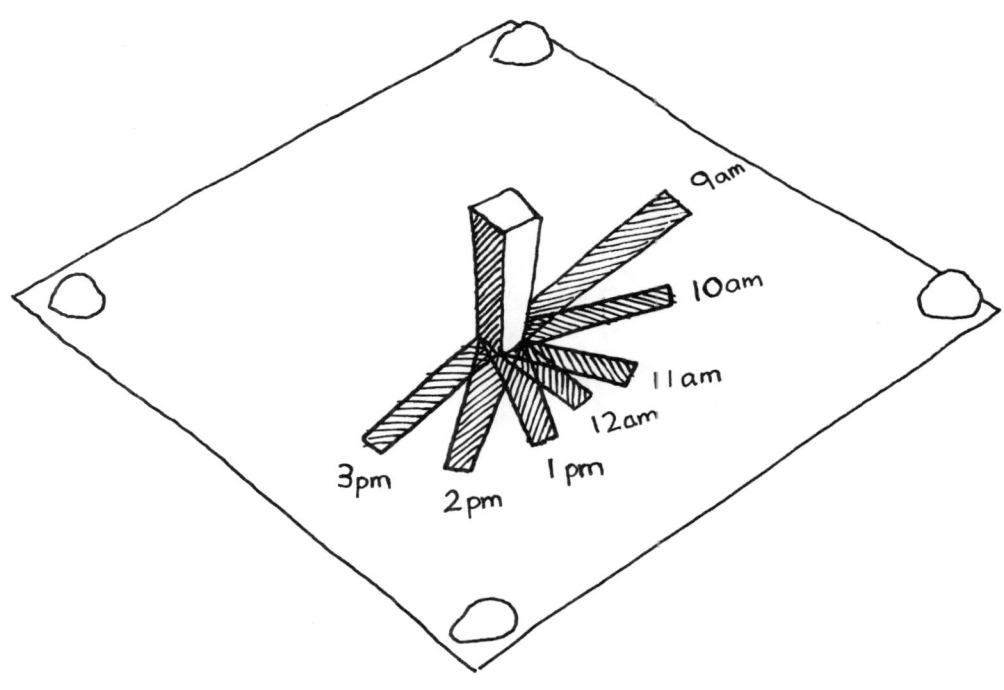

9am

10am

11am

12am

1pm

2pm

3pm

Design a shadow clock which could be used on an indoor window ledge.

95 96

SPECTRUM SCIENCE

Exploring Life and the Environment
levels 1-3